SECOND In COMMAND

The Touch of the Midas

Ronnie L. King, Sr.

Second in Command
The Touch of the Midas

ISBN: 978-1-7372425-8-1
2022 all rights reserved

Ronnie L. King, Sr.
www.RLKingMinistries.org

I dedicate this book to my son Ronnie Jr. my daughter Sharonda, and to my grandchildren Lauryn, and David III. Being your dad and grandpop is my highest honor.

FOREWORD

I've been speaking about magic words which is our superpower; things that we speak, things that we say. When you speak a thing, if there is not hands to bring it together, then the words fall to the ground. The Touch of the Midas is a touch of fortune (gold), the ability to gain success. Gold is also resources, abundance, wealth and relationships. If you can just see beyond the dust and see the actual splendor and the glory of it, you can build the type of relationships that connect you to better resources.

The Touch of the Midas first starts by a vision, he sees something, he says something and then what he says, moves the object or situation. It's no coincidence that his name is King. If a King touches anything just because he is the King, it will cause abundance. For 25 years, this man has been my Midas. To the point if he walks into a room most people look over their shoulder to see who is coming behind him. They are looking for me. The Touch of a Midas is a magical touch of purpose, insight, and foresight. It's the anointing of the Butler. The person who removes the lint off your shoulder. You need to find your Midas for the touch.

Bishop George G. Bloomer

TABLE OF CONTENTS

PREFACE

Let's go on a journey. From the dusty country roads of Goldsboro, North Carolina to speaking on huge platforms, performing on national stages, and being the assistant to a General in the Kingdom, did I know it was going to be like this? Certainly not. I could've only dreamed about what I'm doing now. I had no clue that I was in God's mind to this extent. I am here! It wasn't easy, but working on a farm made me tough and resilient. The farm was my processing chamber to becoming the Second Man to a General in the Kingdom. I have at my fingertips the phone numbers of major players in the Kingdom.

I will share with you some principles and divine secrets of how to serve great men and women of God and uphold the arms of God's Gatekeepers. The ups and downs and ins and outs of learning the correct way was taught to me by experience. Tribulation works patience. Patience works experience. Experience works hope and hope does not disappoint. God turned my shame into Glory. It is written, *"For your shame ye shall have double; and for confusion they shall rejoice in their portion: therefore in their land they shall possess the double: everlasting joy shall be unto them."* Isaiah 61:7 KJV

Follow me on this journey to greatness. Prepare yourself for a journey of a lifetime. Where we are going is full of adventure. Pack your bags, check your brakes and oil, put your seatbelt on check your rear view and side mirrors, and fill the tank up; it's going to be a long trip. While you are following, look at your own situation and see the handy work of God as He molds you into the glorious image of your destiny. God writes all the pages of your life. Your steps are ordered, so trust His order and let the journey begin.

INTRODUCTION

Second in Command – The Touch of the Midas is a story, a lesson, and a journey about how God selects and trains unassuming warriors to assist great Generals in the Kingdom. To get into this position, you must be chosen and qualified to stand behind and assist God's great movers and shakers. How God chooses us is a mystery. What's in His mind when He decides to pick a person? What's His purpose and strategy for training someone when the someone doesn't know he or she is being trained for that position? It doesn't make sense, but it works.

This book shows how God took a test project and developed him into a leader. It wasn't an easy journey. It's not for the faint in heart. It proves that God used the insignificant things to show how great He is. That's just like God. There are many stories in this book, and each story has a lesson. It's a step-by-step manual that covers a period of twenty six years. This book carries us from tragedy to triumph, from rejection to acceptance, from poverty to a state of having more than enough. It shows the transition from a timid servant to a confident leader. Second in Command shows the correlation between the First in Command and the Second in Command and how each role has its own challenges, strategies, its own set of rules and its own language.

Let's go back in time and see how God writes our life and makes us an open book to be read of all men as it is written 2 Corinthians 3:2 *"Ye are our epistle written in our hearts, known and read of all men:"*

Chapter 1

CULTURE SHOCK, I HAD NO CLUE

The Story

It all started in June 1996. There was no Facebook, no Twitter, and no Instagram. It was my daily practice to read the newspaper, the Durham Morning Herald. I was working at a paint company. I had been there for 15 years. I was married and we had two small children. My son was about five years old and my daughter was around seven years old. At that time, we were in the process of leaving our former ministry, but I had no clue what my next church was going to be, so we just waited.

One day I read in the newspaper that a preacher was handcuffed to a tent. I am a nosey person, so this was kind of interesting to me and I wanted to see what that preacher was doing at that tent, that had gotten him handcuffed. That preacher, who was having the tent revival in Durham, North Carolina, was Reverend Bloomer. I hadn't been to a tent revival in years, so my wife and I, and my two children got dressed and went to attend service at the tent. We were the first ones there. We sat down and patiently waited for the service to start.

I'll never forget there was a lady there and she was anxiously waiting on the service to start as well. She grew tired of waiting for the service to start and her impatience took over. She then attempted to go to the microphone and start praise and worship. She began to sing and she looked and saw us sitting in the audience and then invited us to the microphone to help her sing praise and worship. Little did we know that she had no authority to do this. We sang our little hearts out for about 15 minutes. There was a small trailer sitting beside the tent that was used for an office. I saw the trailer door open and out came this preacher. He was the same man I saw in the newspaper, Reverend Bloomer, so tent revival began.

The singing was wonderful as well as very uplifting and then it was time for the word. Reverend Bloomer was preaching that night, so he looked at me sitting in the audience with my family and he called me up and began to speak a word of prophesy to me and said, *"God is going to bring you to another level. New doors are going to open for you."* Well, that was all I needed. I knew that this place was going to be my next level of ministry, but there was no church; there was only a tent. At the close of the tent revival, Reverend Bloomer announced that he would be starting his church July 1, 1996. I knew I had to be there. My wife and I proceeded to resign from our former ministry and start our new adventure.

Well, that day finally arrived, the first Sunday in July 1996, at 101 Corcoran Street Durham, North Carolina. Excitement was in the air. This was the day we were starting our new adventure with our new church and new church family. We were looking forward to having a new spiritual experience, going to a new level, and new opportunities and greater doors.

Service started at 11:00am, so we knew we had to be in place. My wife, son and daughter, and my mother walked into our new church, The Bethel Christian Center. We took a seat and started enjoying the praise and worship. Reverend Bloomer walked in and began to talk about the different facets of ministries that we were going to have. I remember earlier that he said we were going to have at least 70 elders crisscrossing the United States and preaching in different churches. The idea sounded exciting to me and I felt I was ready, after all I had been preaching for five years. This is what I wanted. It was my time, at least I thought, but I had no clue.

Church was over and the journey began. Immediately after benediction, a young man came up to me and introduced himself. He was the musician and asked me to help put up the sound equipment. I quickly agreed and we broke down the sound equipment, locked it up and went home. It was just a great feeling. Bible study was that Tuesday night and we had our pen and paper ready because I knew this man had a lot to say and was very knowledgeable about the scriptures. The first bible study lesson I heard Reverend Bloomer teach was on *"The Lord's Prayer."*

The next Sunday, we attended my former church because we had to say our goodbyes. We were at that church from 1983-1996 and we had developed great relationships. One thing I knew for sure we had to leave right and that's what we did. We wrote a letter stating that we were leaving, and the letter was read in the morning service. Everyone cried and wished us well. Bethel was having an evening service, so we went there that night, but I found out that Reverend Bloomer was out of town that day; a guest preacher was there. It was not a problem, because we were at our new home.

On the third Sunday, in July 1996, my family and I, walked into Bethel Christian center, ready to go forward. After we were seated the Pastor's daughter came and said, "*My Daddy wants to see you.*" Wow, I had never had a conversation with this Pastor. I wondered what he wanted. I followed her to the office and Reverend Bloomer was sitting at his desk looking over a manuscript of a new book he had written entitled, *Witchcraft in the Pews*. Wow! I was honored. As I looked to my left, I saw a large collection of VHS videos where Reverend Bloomer had preached all over the world.

I asked him if I could take a couple of videos home. He said, "*Sure*". I saw one that was from when he was preaching at a Praise Power Conference, titled, "*I'm Not Who I Told You I was.*" We had a short discussion; I told him I was an Evangelist and that I was ready to preach. He said, "*Ok. Pick someone to read the morning scripture and prayer.*" I agreed, then I got ready to leave and before I closed the door, he told me he wanted me to sit in the front section beside the First Lady and him. I was honored and the service was great. After the benediction, we put up the equipment folded up the folding chairs and went home.

As soon as we walked in the house, I popped in the video and there he was ministering in front of 8,000 people at that service and he sang the song, *"I'm in awe of your presence Jesus. I'm in awe of your majesty. You are awesome to me."* I will never forget how I felt. I immediately knew I was at a new level and had a lot to learn about ministry, but I was ready for the challenge. I watched video after video listening and gleaning from sermon to sermon. I was excited about my new adventure. I felt I was ready, but I had no clue.

The Lesson

As leaders we all have intentions of being great. Most leaders want a mansion, a private jet, and to speak to large audiences; that's the leaders dream. What about the person who is to assist the leader? Where do his or her dreams lead them? Will you always be in the shadow of another person or will you be able to create your own shadows? That is something to think about. Can your character handle being Second in Command? Where is your best fit? Sometimes God has to uproot you from one place to put you where He desires you to be and He knows how to do that.

> Sometimes we are hesitant about going forward because of the challenges that face us.

Have you ever been in an unfamiliar territory? This could be a place that you had never been before, or a place in which you are not used. Sometimes we are hesitant about going forward because of the challenges that face us. This New land has giants and we had never fought giants before. We were running from the grasshoppers, and frogs and the Egyptian pests; now we were facing giants. We must remember when we go into a new territory, we must go with a promise, a word or something that we can hold on to until we reach our destination. We must keep our eyes on the end result.

We know that roses have thorns, but it's not the thorns that attract us, it's the blossom. We must be mindful of the thorn. If God made you a promise, then a promise is a promise. You know that His word will not fail. Stay where you are long enough to get a word, or marching orders then you can move with confidence. You can face any obstacle that comes your way, but if you proceed without a word then you will wind up frustrated, discouraged and quit.

ALL of your steps are ordered by the Lord. If you truly believe that then you just walk, trust and His plan will unfold. In the end you will see a well-polished vessel fit for the master's use.

Chapter 2

BOMBSHELL

The Story

When we started going to Bethel in 1996 we were beginning to meet new friends, or so I thought. There were cliques that were out saying, "*New level, new devil.*" I didn't know what that meant. After all, I was a country boy from Goldsboro, NC that was raised in a sanctified church.

I was tutored by older women who adopted me as their own since I was saved at an early age of 16 because I was very serious about my walk with God. I would pray for hours and memorize whole books of the Bible because I had plenty of time. I didn't play with other kids because I thought they were of the devil. They clubbed and partied and went to games. I didn't because all that stuff was worldly, and I knew I would go to hell.

I sat at the house and listened to tapes and memorized the hymn book and the Bible because

I didn't want to miss the rapture. 99 1/2 won't do. All I did was attend church services and revivals every night. I also sang in 5 choirs and attended prayer meetings. I didn't know a lot about Global Ministries, but I knew a lot about church. I was raised in the United Holy Church which I loved dearly, and still do because that was my foundation.

Bethel had about 50 members of which 12 were ministers who felt they all had a ministry. I proceeded to get to know them especially since we were supposed to work together. Because I was the one who chose who did scripture and prayer, I was always trying to find the best fit for the service. Things were good for a while until they started saying I was the Assistant Pastor. I had a problem with that because all I was doing was choosing people to read and pray and helping break down the chairs and music equipment. I mentioned it to Reverend Bloomer, and he said, *"This church is too small to have an Assistant Pastor."*

The church had to go on a bus trip to Salisbury, NC which was about 2 hours away. We all loaded the bus. We had great conversation going there. Reverend Bloomer drove behind the bus. After service was over, we loaded the bus, everyone was seated and someone came on the bus and told me that Reverend Bloomer wanted me to ride back in his car with him and I did, but I left my belongings on the bus. When we got back to Durham, I had to get my belongings off the bus. As I stepped on the bus, it felt like a refrigerator in the atmosphere. What happened? Everyone was looking at me as if to say, "Who do you think you are riding with the Pastor?" After that day, I knew all those relationships had changed and the people who I thought were my friends were just smiling in my face.

Reverend Bloomer had just started preaching about Witchcraft in the Pews; Jealously, Competition and Sabotage. It was at that time, that all of this was manifesting in the church. It was horrible. Everyone was out for blood. At my old ministry, we all grew up together, but here I was meeting a new set of people who were very interesting to say the least. I didn't let that deter me because I didn't need friends. I was raised up by myself on a farm. Back in the woods with no one to play with, I would tend to the farm animals all day. I was perfectly fine, but what I didn't want was to be surrounded by lot of fake friends. I had a job to do, and that job was to do what Reverend Bloomer said. Everyone had agendas, and the cat fights were on.

I really didn't know the Pastor personally

because we never fellowshipped together. I decided to stop by the office after work and talk to him. As I was going to his office door, all I heard was yelling. What was this? What's wrong and why was the man of God yelling? It was none of my business, I guess, but I wasn't about to stick around to find out. I left and went back home. I didn't know Reverend Bloomer had a temper like that. How could a person preach, pastor, and have a temper? I would soon learn. I was a laid-back kind of man, just happy go lucky, and don't worry be happy. I was going to have to talk to Rev. He couldn't be saved and act like that,

The church was starting to grow and I remember one evening after Rev. preached the Lord instructed him to take up a sacrificial offering; I never heard of that. 10 dollars was my limit. He passed out envelopes and members began to put money in the offering. All I put in the envelope was 8 dollars, that was my sacrifice, I felt pretty good about that and went on my merry way. The next Sunday Rev. called a meeting with the men and shut the door and proceeded to say, "*King, I am appalled and insulted. I'm a national preacher leading this church, and I'm bringing you beside me. I'm receiving an offering and all you could give is $8 dollars?*" I was embarrassed. Why did he have to call me out like that? That's all I had. I'm trying to raise a family and he was fussing over $8 dollars. I wasn't right for a while. I got over it and knew I had to come up in my giving. I never went through that at my last church. The next Sunday he asked for everyone to give $20. I was ready and was the first in line, so the journey begins.

We were quickly outgrowing the building and we knew we had to find another place of worship. The first day I drove by the potential new building, it was dilapidated, in a bad neighborhood, and had a lot of trash. The warfare we had trying to get in this building was unbelievable. The opposition was great. Even with all the going back-and-forth to the school board, we finally acquired the building. This new building ended up being on 515 Dowd Street.

We had very few men in church at that time, but we knew we had to get to work to get this building ready for worship. It was going to be a long tedious project, but somebody had to do it. We made a commitment, after work every day to come by the church and do some work. We started cleaning out rooms. I had never seen so much junk in all my life. No problem! We could do it. We were young, strong, focused and determined. It was a few more brothers and me night after night. Hot, cold, early, late whatever it took, we were ready. It took us a whole year to get that building ready, but it still wasn't quite ready for worship.

December 1997, there was a flood in the building on Coughlin Street and we had no place to worship. New Year's Eve 1998, we decided to have church at our new location 515 Dowd St., Durham, NC.

The Lesson

All my life, the people that nurtured me in my walk with the Lord were women. This was the first time that the Lord put a real man in my life, not just a real man, but a man of ministry, authority, a great platform, and a temper sometimes.

(What does your next level look like?)

God must use heat and pressure to develop us to make us into the diamond that he sees in us. I had many talents and gifts that were lying dormant and unnoticed.

When I first came to the church, I didn't have a lot to say, I would just do my job. I didn't make a lot of friends. I was laid-back, kind of shy, and really friendly. I realized that Reverend Bloomer was just the opposite. There was nothing laid-back about this preacher. He always had something to say and would say it, but that's just what I needed in my life for my next level.

What does your next level look like? Who can you take with you? If you bring someone, will they be able to handle where God is carrying you? Many people will speak into your life and tell you where they THINK God is carrying you. If they really saw how high you were going, they would realize that it's too high for them. They would see there's not enough space at that dimension. They would notice that the air is too thin for them, but you would notice it's just right for you. You were built for that level.

You would have to deal with the back lash of you leaving them. People have a way of reminding you, they will say things like, *"When you arrive don't forget me." "Don't forget us little people when you become a big shot." "Oh, he is getting big now."* They would realize they were not going, and they would keep talking because their insecurities would keep speaking. Well, I'm sorry, but I do not have to apologize for my next level. Do I have to keep explaining that over and over?

> If God is allowing you to walk
> with a great leader, you will have to
> come out of the population.

When Jesus went up into the high mountains, he went alone. Be prepared to walk alone. Can you handle that? If God is allowing you to walk with a great leader, you will have to come out of the population. It's important that you understand you are exclusive. If you are serving someone who has bodyguards 24/7, what makes you think that you are not a target also? If they can get to you, then they can get to him. You don't want to be the weakest link.

Many people will try to befriend you. Don't think your popularity is because of you, and everyone is trying to see you. NO! It is the one you are serving. When the crowds in scripture were pressing to see Jesus, the disciples thought they were pressing to see them. It's not about you. It's about the person that you are serving. It's not your time to shine. You are the shadow for now and the only time the shadow is in front of you is when the light is behind you.

Chapter 3

NOW, AIN'T THAT FUNNY

The Story

In 1998, I was appointed a major position in Bethel. I was appointed Pastor of Pastoral Ministries. First of all, I didn't have a clue what that was, but I knew it was something big. So was this like an assistant pastor or something? I was in no position to lead like that. I didn't have a Cadillac or a lot of money in the bank. I couldn't give big offerings or wear designer suits. I had one black suit to be honest, I didn't even buy the suit. Reverend Bloomer bought it for me on a trip to New York City with a few of the brothers in the church. How could I command respect? Who would follow me anywhere when everyone was doing better than me? That didn't stop the process.

Reverend Bloomer would always tell me my tank was filled up with zeal, but God was going to fill my tank with experience and give me an anointing.

What was he talking about? I was already anointed. I was a wonderful preacher or so I thought. I preached at revivals, anniversaries, and other functions, but I never preached on his outgoing platforms. I felt I could do it. After all, I could make people jump and shout. What was he talking about? Soon I would learn, and boy did I learn.

I was in a church of thugs and street people from New York. Men that have been in prison. Men that carried guns and didn't mind using them. I was never a product of the street; I was raised by old women that wore white and spoke in tongues. How could I lead such a group completely opposite of me? Of course, they would proceed to remind me of that. We were at a restaurant and the guys told me I was the weakest link in the men's fellowship because I didn't curse or have a hard background; that kind of bothered me.

Reverend Bloomer would let me preach on Sundays when he was out of town. That was a big deal to me. I would be up all night, adrenaline flowing, and pacing the floor trying to figure out what to preach that the people would enjoy.

Sometimes he would call me when he was out of town and ask me what I was preaching. What nerve, I was preaching what God told me to preach.

One Saturday night he called me and asked me what I was preaching and I said, "I'm preaching *"Shake it Off."* When Paul shook off the snake in the Book of Acts and felt no harm. I felt that was a good message, but nooooo it was not good enough. He proceeded to fuss and ask me *"What are you talking about? Why are you preaching about a snake?* What is biting you?" Then he said to me *"Get another topic or I will get somebody else and put them in your spot. Now, when I call back you better have something."* Wow, that wasn't good enough and I had worked on that message all night. Back to the drawing board. I preached that Sunday, *"Only God can be God"* and it went over well.

During those days, we had what you would call Bloomerites. These were the people that when they found out Rev. was out of town, they would come and leave, call their friends and tell them not to come, and they would make themselves known that they were Bloomerites. We would hear them. They didn't want to hear anyone, but the pastor. How could you command a group of people who weren't interested in hearing you at all? Oh well, he kept putting me up to preach and when it was over he didn't mind telling me if I did well or if I did horribly. He would always tell me the offering was down $5000 dollars. The people were shouting, but they weren't giving, but he always kept putting me up. I don't know why because I didn't think he liked me.

He was always mad about something, and people were always blaming me for stuff going wrong, like they had it in for me. I kept my head up.

Nobody knows the work I put into that building; painting, putting up sheet rock, wallpaper, and tearing down walls, all long night after night while my family was barely surviving at home. Some nights we hauled junk all night long. We were in one end of the building and there were people stealing paint out of the other end. We had to do like Nehemiah, work and fight.

It took us almost a whole year to get that building ready for worship with very little help from the guys who said I was the weakest link. Nobody had a problem with me banging on nails and painting, but soon as I got the in pulpit and started talking, they had a problem. Was God training me to be a Pastor of Pastoral Ministries? If he was, then it didn't feel good. Why didn't He just anoint me and send me forth? Why did I have to go through all that hell? I didn't bother anybody, but that didn't stop them.

One day I was sleep in the church van, and a group of people were standing beside the van talking about me. You wouldn't believe who it was, these were the very ones in my face talking about how much of a blessing I was. What a hypocrisy, but I kept my focus for a while.

We had meeting after meeting, all night long, with fussing and fighting. Some nights, I left the meeting just in time to go to work. What was God doing? What did he have in mind? This really was not funny. I could've stayed at my old church where things were comfortable for me and where they liked me. Why all this trouble? Could I just live a normal life without all the drama?

One night I drove up to church and heard Rev fussing at the musician. OMG! I kindly got back in my car and drove back home. Ain't nobody got time for that. God, what are you doing? I didn't ask for this. This is certainly a new level and new devil.
I wasn't use to it, and I had never had it in my mind to quit because I was not a quitter. I was going to see what the end was going to and it wasn't looking too good at the moment.

The Lesson

What does it take to help a great man of God? A lot of people like the glamour of it all and the attention. There's something about power that makes people go crazy. People will fight like cats and dogs just to have a position. When you get a position, you must bring leadership to it. Respect cannot be demanded; it has to be commanded. You command respect by the way you posture and present yourself, the way you speak, the way you sit, and the way you dress.

(A second man must be in step or in sync with the first man.)

Reverend Bloomer would begin teaching series and it was amazing because when he started teaching, it would always manifest. The training that it took to be a second man was not easy. A second man must be in step or in sync with the first man. That is not easy if the two come from two totally different walks of life. There are two separate experiences, ideologies, and backgrounds.

Chapter 4

COVENANT BREAKER

The Story

In 1999, three years after the church started, we were having a growth spurt. The church was growing like wildfire. We had worked three years to bring the building up to par. Ministries were being established. We had a functioning Choir, Usher Board, and Parking Crew. The Band was in place and the church was running like a well-oiled machine. This was great. I had just been promoted to Pastor of Ministerial Ministries. Things were looking up. The future in ministry was promising. It looked like things were progressing fast. Bishop was traveling out of the pulpit 20 days out of the month. He would leave the church for me to hold together and I was doing a pretty good job at that time.

We decided to celebrate Bishop's birthday. We had all members to give bishop $100 dollars and that was a success. We had around 200 members. We celebrated on a Sunday night, and immediately after the celebration, Bishop came to the podium and thanked everyone for coming and supporting, and after his speech he called me to the pulpit. Okay, was I going to get rebuked for something? What did I do? He told the congregation how faithful I had been, and he proceeded to reach in his pocket and pull out this little box. Inside the box was a ring. He said, *"This ring represents covenant and now we are in covenant with one another."* The whole church started clapping; people were crying. It was a phenomenal time. It was a night I would never forget. Never in my life had I been so honored. He really did like me.

I put the ring on and wore it like a king. When I would lift my hand to praise the Lord, I would use the hand with the ring. We were in covenant; I was now connected to greatness, and no one could deny it. *Acts 4:13* tells a story about how the people had recognized the disciples were ignorant and unlearned men, but the scriptures say that they took notice that they had been with Jesus. Look at who I'm with now.

As time progressed my life in ministry was flourishing, but my private life was a failure. Finances were out of whack and my relationship was failing. Could it get any worse? My wife and I, at that time were strapped for cash: little food to eat, car was on the blimp, with two children to feed.

I needed to really up my game as being a provider. Not only that, I needed some quick cash. I just needed one hundred dollars, so I looked around to see how could I get one hundred dollars, and then I remember the ring. If it was worth thousands, at least I could get one hundred for it. I would get it back in a week or so. Nobody would know. Without any thought, I pawned the ring got the hundred dollars and that was that or was it.

A few days had passed, and we were having a service and Bishop noticed I was praising like I normally would, but not with the ring hand. He called me in the office and proceeded to ask me *"Where was the ring?"* I said, I put it in the safe for safe keeping. He said, *"Ok, but where was the ring?"* I said it was at the house. He got up out the chair and went and closed the door and asked again. *"Where was the ring?"*

I knew he knew something was wrong. I finally told him what happened. He sighed shook his head and said, *" If you needed a hundred dollars, you could've asked me and I would've given it to you. What you did, was broke the covenant."* I thought, what was all the fuss about. It was just a ring.

Well, from that day forward, for about five years things went downhill. I mean week after week something was happening; it was then I realized what I had done. The men were laughing at me and said they wished they got a ring. I would hear that for years until the all those men had left the church. It was then that I realized that we all had broken the covenant. I just stayed.

The Lesson

In order to assist a leader in ministry or any entity in life, there must be a type of bond. Some may call it covenant. Twenty years later, the covenant was restored. Now, I reach out to all the other men from time to time to tell my story of how, like Samson; my hair grew back. Get your covenant restored with your leader. Then you will receive the anointing that is supposed to flow. The ring was a symbol of the covenant that was made in the heart. Without a covenant, there is no trust. When there is no trust, secrets can't be kept. If you can't keep a secret, then you can't be trusted with confidential information.

When you are working in ministry, you are working with people and if you are working with people then there will be secrets and things that don't need to be shared. Assistants sometimes know more secrets than the Pastor because in order to get to the Pastor you have to go through the assistant. If the assistant can't be trusted, then there is no bond. If there is no bond, the people will see it because it will be obvious. You can't hide a disconnection.

(Bonds and covenants
don't happen overnight.)

If a light switch is bad in your house, then everyone will notice it. You will flip the switch and nothing will happen. You will have to call an electrician to fix the disconnection, a person who is skilled to sense and detect disconnections. Bonds and covenants don't happen overnight. You can't force them. If you're not a good fit, then you will have to find where you fit.

The assistant should be so well connected to his leader that when the people see the assistant, they know a few steps behind him will be his leader. Bishop once told me, *"Don't go everywhere because when people see you, they automatically look for me."* You don't want to be everywhere. Watch where you go and who you hang out with. We must not bring shame or a reproach to the ministry.

Chapter 5

THE BALANCING ACT

The Story

In our early church years, we were very young. The fame of Bishop Bloomer was spreading uncontrollably. He was growing and growing and growing. His wisdom was like the wisdom of Solomon. Wisdom came from his lips like honey out of a honeycomb and people from all over the world were amazed at how he could resolve conflict especially how he handled scandals in our church and the churches abroad. How could I assist such a great leader? I wasn't that smart, I wasn't that anointed, didn't have a great vocabulary, and never traveled anywhere, but to Disney World in Florida. What did he need me for?

He would go to great conferences and have me sit beside him. I looked like a bump on a log compared to such a great orator and statesman, and of course the people said the same thing. After all, I was a country cornball from Goldsboro. What did I have to say that would cause anyone to listen to me? The Bible says,

> *"For I know the thoughts that I think toward you, saith the Lord, thoughts of peace, and not of evil, to give you an expected end."*
>
> *Jeremiah 29:11 KJV*

God has a way of taking the simple things and confounding the wise. Man looks on the outward appearance, but God looks at the heart. Know that I'm 10 times bigger on the inside than I am on the outside. How was I to assist this giant of a preacher? What in the world was Bishop thinking to even try to use me in any fashion? He would put me up and I would do the dumbest things. How could I be so stupid?

One Sunday, we had Minister's Class upstairs with about 20 in attendance. I was teaching the class. I decided to combine my class with the other class which was a class on Evangelism. After all, we all supposed to be evangelists. There's nothing wrong with that or so I thought. In the combined class, we had a great discussion. There was only one problem.

I didn't get permission. The Lord led me to do it and I felt the minister's needed it. The class was over and that was that.

The next Sunday, Bishop Bloomer cooked dinner for the leaders and the food was wonderful. After we finished eating and sat down, He proceeded to say, *"Nothing is to be done in my church without my permission and that you overstepped my boundaries."* All eyes were on me. Let's go down the list: First Lady, my wife, my mother, my brother, all the ministers that were in my Minister's Class and all my haters were present. All eyes were on me. I never felt such pressure in all my life.

He opened the floor for me to speak, but instead of speaking, I got choked up and couldn't speak. Everyone kept watching as to say you are finished now. I just knew this country bumpkin wasn't going to make it. There was a vote in the room whether I was to remain the Pastor of Ministerial Ministries and the vote was unanimously yes. I was shocked because I was so ready to quit. I didn't need all this pressure. I just wanted to serve my leader as I had in the past. Oh well, let's try it again.

Less than a week later, I was right back in the hot seat. Luck was not on my side. Trying to play the balancing act of a marriage that was falling apart while trying to work in ministry is not fun. It was not an easy task, but I never gave up. Maybe I should have because it wasn't working.

I worked at a paint company for 15 years and never missed one day of work in fifteen years. I never called out. I was never sick or anything. I was growing in the company. They would give me the deposit bag to put in the bank after work, which I did for fifteen years.

This one evening, I just threw it in the glove compartment one Friday and didn't take it. I was planning on taking it Saturday, but I didn't. I also put Saturday's bank deposit in the same compartment; I was going to drop it off before the bank opened on Monday morning. On Monday morning, I was getting in the car and noticed the compartment was opened and all the cash was taken from the bank deposit bags, but the checks were left. When I saw this, my heart dropped; I was petrified. Who broke in my car and took the cash? Who even knew that the deposits were in there? Now I'm in trouble. $30,000 was missing from the bags and what was I going to do? I didn't have that kind of money to replace it. I had to think of a plan do what I would do was volunteer to take all bank deposits to bank and would take the cash from that day and put in the previous day, so no one would notice. It worked for a while. I was about to have a nervous breakdown because of the pressure. I didn't mention it to anyone.

This lasted for two months until I woke up one morning and my whole face was twisted. I had to preach at our Raleigh location. I wasn't in pain; I just thought it would go away, but it got worse. I preached anyway and the service was fantastic. When I got back to the Durham church, the saints saw me and made me go to the Emergency Room. I found out I had Bell's Palsy and this was due to the stress of the whole ordeal. I had to go to work with a twisted face because if I missed then the missing money would be found out. I continued to push myself.

Then one day, in September 1999, the police came and arrested me from my job and took me to jail. I was scheduled to preach that Sunday morning. Bishop Bloomer got me out of jail. He called me and never ridiculed me. He just said, "*Let me put someone else up to preach because we don't know who knows about this.*" He also said, "*Sit in the pulpit and hold your head up. We're going to get through this.*" You know because of this, I had no job and my marriage was over. Can you blame her? Who wanted to be married to a thief?

Nobody believed I didn't take the money, but Bishop Bloomer believed me. I made up in my mind that day I was going to stick with him come hell or high water.

If God has a plan for you, then remember your steps are ordered.

The Lesson

Now my tank was being filled with experience and not zeal. God worked a miracle because after 2 years of waiting on my court date, the police officer who arrested me never came to give his report, so the court dismissed the charges. I had witnessed a miracle in my life. If God has a plan for you, then remember your steps are ordered. Even good steps, bad steps, missteps, and wrong steps are all ordered. I was glad I had someone in my corner who believed in me.

Chapter 6

TENT MASTER

The Story

What do you do when you are waiting on your ministry to come to prominence? Do you just sit around and twiddle your thumbs? I always wanted to work in full time ministry, but didn't have the faith to just launch out. How do you get paid if people decide not to pay their tithes and offering? How do you survive if your leader dies or a major scandal breaks out?

Preachers live by begging literally. My mind went back to the old, sanctified church where I could hear the Pastor begging for one more dollar to buy a microphone really? Had it come to that? How was I going to live off of one dollar? I didn't know about this full-time ministry stuff.

Since the incident that happen with my job, I was sat down quietly until the outcome. I was not used to just sitting down doing nothing. I was a vibrant youthful man full of energy and to just sit still would kill me; I had to do something. One day, we had a men's fellowship meeting and Bishop Bloomer announced that we would be buying an old Kmart building and it needed to be cleaned out and he asked for volunteers. Well, everyone looked around. That's too much work. Bishop looked at me said, "*I know the perfect person to oversee this project.*" And he said "*King I want you to do this.*" Here we go again. Didn't we just get finished getting our sanctuary ready with little or no help? Now this, but I guessed it was something to do.

I rallied all the men together and there were about 30 men that came to the building on the first night. There was hope. The building was about 30,000 square feet of space. It was full of shelves, and we had to break them down and put them in a truck. It started out good for about 2 days. Then the third day, I was waiting on the men to arrive, but no one showed up, but one of the Deacons and a church Mother. Where were the brothers at? We started taking shelves apart. Finally, the men arrived; we got help. Really???

They congregated in the front of the building and proceeded to talk about basketball and we had one brother who wanted to pray for everyone's safety. Now, we had a problem with that, because he was the clumsiest one out there. He was always falling off ladders and stepping in paint buckets. I told him he needed to pray for himself because we were fine. After a few months, we finished the old Kmart building. I figured I was back ready for the pulpit. Ready to preach, ready to go to the world, and maybe one day have a private jet, but not yet.

Bishop announced that he was having a tent revival for 20 days. That was exciting to me! Church outside! When does it start? The tent revival sounded like fun. The problem was we had to set up the tent. Did I hear him correctly? We didn't know how to set up a tent.

We had a men's meeting, and we had a lot of men in the church now. It was upwards of about 100 men and with 100 men we should've able to do it. Bishop purchased a tent and one of the Deacons showed me how to put it up. I had all the brothers to come help put it up. We had about 10 brothers to come. Where were the other 90? I kind of felt like Jesus when he said, *"Where are the nine?"* The tent revival was on. 20 days of wind, heat, rain, hurricane, but services were awesome. I had done it again and everyone called me Tent Master.

My marriage was on the rocks during these times. It was full of fussing and arguing. One afternoon, I was preparing to go to the tent and had an altercation at home and the police were called, just for arguing. Well, off to jail I went. Here we go again.

The next night under the tent people were falling out in the spirit, so I proceeded to help one lady. I got out of my seat and walked to the alter. Bishop said *"Sit down."* I was shocked and everyone heard it, so I went and sat down. Why? What did I do? I had to take 10 weeks of anger management classes, but I was not violent and never would be, but I took the classes. What was God doing? What was all this about? I really liked this church, but it was getting to be a little too much.

One night there was a hurricane, so I slept in the tent trailer to guard the equipment. While the wind was blowing, I heard gunshots. I proceeded to look out the window and I saw a young man run out of the corner store and collapse. He died on the scene. I was a witness, but no one saw me in the trailer, and I wasn't about to reveal myself. Those were growing years for me.

Bishop Bloomer decided to go an extra 5 nights at the tent after 20 days of rain. I wanted to start putting some stuff up early; I had a large truck ready. My son and I were going to take down some small tents, so we could get a head start on breakdown. As I was backing the truck up, I knocked down the light pole that supplied power to the tent. Well, the tent revival was over.

That was one year, we disobeyed the Lord. I was disappointed. I ran back to church to tell Deacon that I knocked down the tent and he smiled and said *"Thanks."* We told Bishop Bloomer and he said, *"Praise the Lord."* Why was I the only one upset? I guess all good things must come to an end voluntarily or involuntarily and that's that.

Lesson

Tent revival became the norm. When other ministries heard of our success in doing tent revival, they wanted to jump on board. They figured if they would just put up a tent that people would automatically just appear under the tent and that was not the case. In order to have a successful tent crusade, you have got to have proper advertising. That means you've got to spend some money on billboards, television commercials, flyer campaign, and so many more outlets.

> Experience is the greatest teacher
> hands down.

I realize that, then you had to determine what the drawing card would be that would entice the people to come sit in the heat for 2 hours. Otherwise, you will just have a few homeless people coming to the service just to receive a fish or hotdog plate. Tent revivals meant work. In order to have a successful tent revival, the grounds had to be clean, free of bugs and mosquitoes and pests. The music had to be state of the art which meant paying musicians to assure that the sound was on point. All of this cost money, upwards of ten to twenty thousand dollars. All of this I learned while overseeing the tent. Now I had Intel and when people called me and asked me about tent meetings, I could correctly advise them on the pros and cons of having a tent meeting. Experience is the greatest teacher hands down. This was another notch in my belt on becoming second in command.

Chapter 7

LODE BAR

The Story

Have you ever been in a place where there was no word, no sound, and no communication? Why does God take you there and leave you there? What was he trying to accomplish? This was a lonely place. There's no encouragement, no praise, and no one calling your name. You were always skipped over by mistake. They would always say they didn't mean any harm, they just forgot to put your name on the list. God, what are you doing and why are you treating me like this? During my roughest days I had to pull strength from within.

From 1999 to 2003, I was in a place of no word. I really mean no word. Whenever a prophet would come to our church for a prophetic conference, I knew for certain I was going to get a word of direction, or encouragement or something to let me know I was on the right road. Anything would have been encouraging, Lord anything. Didn't you see me?

I was living in a boarding house, yes a boarding house. The house was about four miles from the church. I didn't have any transportation because my license was suspended, due to a failure to appear in court on traffic charges. I thought I could just pray them away, but then the cops came and got me off my job again. Even then I had favor with God. My manager gave me my check early because he knew I would need it and he told me my job was secure. Imagine being such a good worker that your company doesn't want to lose you when life's crisis happens. Now that's favor and not only that when my bond was set the check that my manager gave me was just enough to pay the bondsman.

When God is setting you up for something big, you must understand the depth of the trials you have to go through. All you need is endurance, the ability to last and not to give up. I didn't get any encouragement because no one knew what I was going through. People were still jealous of my position, but they didn't know my state. Sometimes God hides things from them because when he brings you out no one will be able to get the credit.

During those times, I didn't have a car. I had to

walk everywhere. I didn't have enough money to catch the bus. The bus fare was only $1.00 and $2.00 you could ride all day. Could you imagine that? I couldn't find 2.00. What in the world? We were singing songs like your blessings knocking at the door *"Your blessings ringing a bell. Do yourself a favor open the door and let it in."* Nice song, but I couldn't find the door.

People in the church were buying houses, cars, and getting financial blessings. It was a wonderful year. Oh really, then why was I catching a cab to and from church? I wasn't about to ask anyone for help, especially church folks. That just wasn't in my character. I just made it the best way I could.

We had a prophetic conference. The prophets were on target that night. I just knew I was going to get a word. I got in line and the line was moving fast; I was the second in line. The lady in front of me fell out in the spirit and I had to catch her. I took her to the side then other people started falling out, so all the rest of the night I was catching people, so I never got my word. How disappointing that was, but I managed to pull myself together and encourage myself and move on.

When Bishop was out of town they used to call me to preach. For two years no one called. Had I lost something? Was I that bad? I know I had made a lot of mistakes, but I was willing to admit my wrongs. I would think, "Hey, can y'all see me? I'm over here? Am I invisible or something?" Oh well, at least I had my job.

(You have to deal with loneliness because ministry is a lonely place.)

The Lesson

When God is trying to make something great out of you, He has to carry you through great storms. You have to deal with loneliness because ministry is a lonely place. People don't call you unless they need something. You have to deal with rejection, even Jesus was despised and rejected. You have to deal with ridicule. All of these are for your making and if you learn these things you will be able to stand.

God gave me a strategy to help me, keys concepts and ideas. Tools that I could use for the rest of my life. I was so glad he took me around about way cause now when I talk to people with a lot of questions I have answers and I understand where they are coming from. I have been under, so I can stand. I didn't know God was training me to be the Second Man. I just knew things in my life weren't correct, and I needed things to get better.

Why the intense pressure? Now I understand, because when the pressure is on me, I don't break down or have melt downs. I just go somewhere, get quiet and when I do that it allows me to focus on the problem at hand and it is then that I'm able to come up with an answer.

The route to this position wasn't easy, but it was worth it and I'm grateful for every moment of testing. Now when challenges come, I can pull from a repertoire of experiences to get me through every storm.

Chapter 8

PASTOR CAN'T DO NO WRONG

The Story

Bishop Bloomer covered me so many times when my behind was showing. A lot of times we feel a draft, but don't know where it's coming from. It's your behind and it's showing. Many times, Bishop Bloomer had to get his hands dirty to come save me, and the people would ridicule him for doing so. He did what he did because of love and thank God for that.

Now people will come to me and say Bloomer this and Bloomer that and I would say that can't be so because of such and such and would set the record straight and the people would actually trust my word and because of it remain loyal to their leader. If I was an evil person, I would add fuel to the fire and God would not be pleased, and that would bring swift judgment on myself. Even if I knew he did it, I would deny it. I don't know what you are talking about; you're mistaken and because of that God gives me grace in these days.

There was a time in my life that I was very lawless. He sat me down for a second time. I was done with this leadership mess; it wasn't worth the trouble. I thought it's my life and I can live it like I want, but I forgot that it was written,

> *"For ye are bought with a price: therefore glorify God in your body, and in your spirit, which are God's."*
>
> *1 Corinthians 6:20 KJV*

I wanted a refund. I never had a chance to party and get high and club all night. My family kept me from that when I was growing up. As soon as I turned 16, I got my driver's license. I had 2 cars a 1979 Buick Skylark and 1982 Buick Duce and a Quarter; I was ready to get my groove on and ready to do my thing. Lo and behold I went to a Revival with Apostle Johnny Washington and got saved. There goes the club because then my whole purpose was to not go to hell because I was headed there quick, fast and in a hurry.

At 35 years old, I was ready to make up for lost time. I missed church for two Sundays because I was tired of this church thing. One night, Bishop drove up to my house at 2:00am in a burgundy van. Was this man crazy? He sat me down, was about to throw me out the church and then he showed up at my house. I was thinking what did he want now? I really didn't like him and I didn't think he liked me.

He let other people get away with murder and would cuss me out for picking the wrong song for choir to sing. God, you had to be kidding me. He sat out in my driveway in a Burgundy Ford van and blew the horn. My neighbors had to hear it. What nerve?

I got in the van, he talked with me till daybreak. He told me he had someone to follow me, so he could keep me alive. Wow! No greater love hath no man than this. That a man would lay down his life (money) for his friend and I had to go to work.

That was the night that changed the course of my life and I have never gone back to that dark place again. I still had a long way to go to get to the place that God had intended for me. I knew I had to protect this man at all costs and I knew I had to be loyal, serve and cover in any capacity that I could.

The Lesson

The job of the Assistant to the Pastor was to cover the Pastor's nakedness as in the case of Noah and his three sons. After the great flood in Genesis, there were only eight people saved. Noah preached 120 years and could only save his family and the animals. Immediately after this, Noah went back to his old ways, drinking. He got drunk and was laying naked in his tent. His sons saw him, and took a blanket and covered him, and because the 2 sons covered him and said they were going to be great because of what they did, cover their father. Was their father drunk? Yes. Was he naked? Yes. Did he do it? Yes, he was guilty, and they caught him.

> You have to realize that your Pastor is just as human as you are.

Today, this would be plastered all over Facebook and social media and it would be a major scandal. When the scandal breaks, normally it's someone within the circle that leaked the info. Cursed be that person who uncovers their leader. You not only uncover him, but you're causing the people who have faith because of him to lose heart. You will not escape judgement if you allow that to happen, because God loves His people. You have to realize that your Pastor is just as human as you are. Normally, they are more flawed because of the anointing that's on their life. It's the Assistants job not to expose, but to cover.

Chapter 9

GOD WHAT ARE YOU UP TO?

The Story

Bishop finally let me travel with him on his private jet. Oh, this was going to be fun. I finally got my lucky break. I packed my suitcase, put on some shorts, and headed to the airport. The first thing he did was look at me and then told me to change clothes. I could do that.

Now, I was flying around the world with the man of God to whatever city you could name; we flew there. Was it fun? Let's talk about it. Bishop's grandson was 6 years old and was traveling also and he was full of energy. Now imagine this was a private jet full of game systems, controllers and PlayStations and all kind of gadgets. He had so many toys we had to figure out where to put the suitcases. We were always leaving stuff on the planes and in the hotel rooms. That answers that question. What was God up to? I didn't know, but I guess He had a plan.

In order to serve great leaders, you have to have patience. I mean for real. Many nights I would take Bishop home and he would say wait in the truck; I'm coming right back out. I would just sit there one to two hours then I would doze off and wake up the next morning. I can't believe I sat here all night. I could have just drove home, but the problem was I had his truck so I was still stuck and couldn't go anywhere because he might call at any minute and decide to go.

I got smart and when he said, "Wait out here." I would say the truck is going to be here, but I was going home, and I would get a ride home. I was not tying up my whole day waiting for him to come out the house. Again, I asked the question what was God up to? I still didn't know, but this wasn't funny.

Now I loved to go shopping with Bishop because he really knows how to shop. Here we go again. We would pick up his grandkids and go to all the toy stores and candy shops. All day I'm walking back and forth to the car taking bags and ordering food. Now, was this how you serve the Man of God? That's how I got in because nobody else wanted to do that. Especially on Friday and Saturday night, those were date nights, but I didn't have a date. I didn't even have a life.

I tagged along listening to Bishop talk, teach, and rebuke day in and day out. I was eventually working my way in to serving the Man of God and learning his ways and his movements and his thoughts. What was God up to? I was starting to figure it out, little by little. It was unfolding. God was training me in the wilderness to serve in the palace.

The Lesson

If you are aspiring to serve a great Man or Woman of God, then God has got to give you on the job training and skills and tactics because one day you are going to serve in excellence. You don't know how big your leader is going to get. While God is developing him, He must develop you also to be able to serve him in a greater capacity.

People always want to sit at the Bishop's feet. Oh really? People fly from across the country to visit and view from afar. From afar, it looks glamourous, and people will sell their houses and property and get a one way ticket to Durham, NC thinking it's going to be peaches and crème. They will come and say," *The*

Lord sent me here to sit at your feet?" Did the Lord show them what the feet looked like?

Being a mentee doesn't mean you hang out with the mentor all day playing golf and eating at fine restaurants talking about the Bible all day. There is a reason that you need a mentor. A person needs a mentor because something is lacking in the area of character, finances, personal development, etc. and things need to be corrected.

It's not fun and games; it's development and growth.

A personal trainer would be considered a mentor, but he has to take you through the course of pain to develop muscles in order to get the physique he or she is desiring. There is soreness for days that causes discomfort in the area of development. Likewise, in the spiritual realm there must be pain and discomfort in the areas of development.

I tell people, "It's not fun and games; it's development and growth." If you think it's fun and games to just sit at his feet and serve the man of God. If you think he is just going to pray for you, prophecy over your life, maybe give you a couple dollars, or that he might even buy you a car, I hate to disappoint you, but it is not like that. That's really the fantasy, of super deep spiritual people who don't want do the work and who want to hang out in Lala land all day.

The truth of the matter is it's just the opposite. It's work because Bishop always needs something. He is always breaking something, always cooking, and so that means somebody must do the shopping, prepping, serving, and cleaning. Where are the spiritual and deep people now? Nowhere to be found.

We ask the Lord to use us for His glory and wait for an anointing to fall on us and knock us to the floor. We think we are going to see visions and dreams. The fact of the matter is, when we ask God to use us, He puts a broom in our hand and tell us to clean the bathroom. I can't believe I'm doing this as anointed as I am. I should be preaching in a conference or something instead I was walking behind the Man of God and carrying his bags. That's how I felt.

I had always wanted to serve in that capacity; that position was full he had men to open his door, get his clothes, and carry his briefcase. I guess there's nothing else for me to do, after all I was a nobody. Who would want me to carry their briefcase? What I would do? Watch others, and if there's one thing I'm good at is observing how things operate and how things click. I could figure out anything and it only would take me a few days and I could replace you because I would study you and figure out what makes you tick. I just hung around even in my days of being sat down, that's exactly what I did, sit down. Ok, you don't want me in the office, I don't have to be in the office. Just put me a chair right outside the office door and I would sit there all day.

There are going to be times in your walk with God that no one will notice you, will call your name, and that's exactly what happened to me. People were just doing things just because they had the power to do it. That's not right. That's evil. I knew my assignment. I was not deterred, and I kept my focus.

We are supposed to be serving God. It is written,

> "What shall we then say to these things? If God be for us, who can be against us?"
>
> *Romans 8:31 KJV*

You may be going through the exact same thing right now. Just know there is a better day coming and you shall receive your reward and they will get theirs. God's plan will prevail in your life, if you put Him first. I hope that you know that your steps are ordered by the Lord. Please take heed and remember, that your greatest deliverance will be the deliverance from what people think.

Chapter 10

IT IS WHAT IT IS

The Story

O ne Sunday morning, we had just got our cameras and we were just starting to record the services. Bishop had stated earlier in the week that he did not want any gum chewing in the church because it would get all over the chairs and that wouldn't be good. That was that and we all understood that.

The following Sunday we were in our 11 am service. During the Praise and Worship, I was in the pulpit sitting directly beside Bishop Bloomer as I always sat. Service was going well. I was really feeling my position of Pastor of Ministerial Ministries. An Usher walked up to me and gave me a tissue and told me to tell Bishop to take the gum out of his mouth. Well, I'm standing beside him feeling myself not paying attention to the situation, took the tissue and turned to Bishop and said, "*The*

Usher said take the gum out of your mouth." Bishop looked at me, looked at the Usher, grabbed my hand and pushed it away. At that point, the Usher saw that Bishop was angry and she gently turned and walked away. What just happened? Did I really allow that to happen, if we weren't on camera? I'm sure that would've been really bad, but the camera saved me that morning.

We went on with the service and the service was phenomenal. I mean it was something going on. People were falling out, screaming, crying and getting delivered like crazy. Oh my God, it was like heaven on earth.

Immediately after the service, Bishop was angry and he went straight up to his office and slammed the door. Everyone heard him yelling, they wanted to know what was wrong with Bishop and I said I don't know. Then he called me in the office and let me have it. When he finally calmed down, he said, *"Go get that Usher!"* We had a meeting and we knew that it was an assignment of the enemy to frustrate his purpose. The devil decided to use the Assistant and the Head Usher, but that spirit was broken that day. The scripture says,

> *"Them that sin rebuke before all, that others also may fear."*
>
> *1 Timothy 5:20 KJV*

Trust me, I had a greater respect for my leader that day. To this day, we still talk and laugh about those days of mistakes and learning. Those days were very important because of the position I hold today. Respect is the key. It is what it is.

The Lesson

As we learn to flow with our Apostle, Prophet, Pastor to assist him or her in ministry, we must learn how they tick. We have to know what frustrates them and what causes them not to be at their best. When we learn this, when they are frustrated, it won't be because of us. A lot of times leaders are derailed or frustrated because of the one who is closer to them. We have his/her ear. The Usher is at the door. The Deacon is in the office and the Choir is in the choir stand. The Parking Attendant is outside, but his attendants are normally right behind him or right beside him and his eye is always on his attendants because he's always giving direction.

The service is always changing and there are always shifts. If the Assistant or Attendants are unfocused or not paying attention, it could cause a train wreck in the service. When that happens, everyone will look at the conductor, the Leader. A good Assistant is always looking to cover the leader, but because of the position, the glamour of the position of Attendant, Executive Pastor, Assistant, Adjutant or Armor bearer, there is always a spirit of pride that sneaks in unaware and chokes the discernment of the Assistant. This is not good because now the attention is on them.

"
.

(A servant is not greater than his Lord)

There is the story in the bible where the people were thronging to get to Jesus and hear him. The disciples said, *"Lord they crying out to us."* Huh? Are you serious? Do you really think they are crying out for you? Are you delusional? I can't believe what I just heard? Do you actually believe that the people really are crying after you? That's got to be a spirit, and a bad one at that.

Let the Pastor stay gone from his pulpit for four consecutive Sundays and see what happens. You will find out what the real deal is. The people stop coming, the offering starts going down. It's not about you, and you better remember that. A servant is not greater than his lord. There will be a time for you to shine, but not now. You must wait until your leader goes up. As in the case if Elijah and Elisha, he couldn't receive double until his master was caught up. Going up doesn't always mean dying, it could mean he has to wait till his master is promoted. Until then you have to know your place and your place is to assist. Do not make government decisions or try to usurp authority. The people want to hear their leader. It is what it is.

Chapter 11

CURTAINS UP

The Story

In 2000, my son was 10 years old and my daughter was 14. Bishop announced that he was going to be preaching at Manpower in St. Petersburg, Florida and he wanted to do an illustrated sermon. That was great and I decided to bring my kids to drama rehearsal, so they could be a part of the ministry. I would bring them after school and let them practice. I didn't think they were so interested, but at least they had something to do.

I was sitting in the audience watching the rehearsal, when the director came to me and said that they needed an old man act in the play. I said, " *Ok, I will help find someone.*" Then he proceeded to say Bishop wanted me to play an old man. Are you serious, an old man? I didn't think so, but I would stand in just this once until we could find someone.

I jumped up on stage and did a try out. The whole cast and all the people present were floored. They were laughing and falling on the floor, some were crying and running to the bathroom. Bishop was laughing, so hard he was face down on the chairs. What in the world was going on? The director would throw out words and I would act them out and the cast was amazed at what was happening. "Oh my God", was what the director said, "This was the missing piece of our production." He said, "Your stage name is Deacon Grey. " What was he talking about? I am not trying to be in any play acting silly. I was an Elder.

The next night Bishop came to me and said, "*I want you to be a part of the drama.*" Now, these were the years that I was really not as involved because my focus was off and I kind of wanted to go in another direction. I wasn't preaching or anything, I was just a regular attendee. When Bishop asked me to be a part of the drama, I told him that it would hurt my ministry. He looked at me and stated, "*What ministry? You can't preach. Get your behind up on that stage and act in this play.*" Out of respect for him, I did.

Bishop was interested in putting a play on the road. We rehearsed a play called *"When Loving You is Wrong."* We did a five night showing at the church and the church was packed each night. This was the play Bishop decided to take on the road.

In 2002, Bishop brought a lady from Atlanta to watch the play to see if it would make it in theatre. That Sunday night, we had to show the play to her. We invited the church out to be the audience, and it was curtains up. We started to perform and because of the bright lights, we couldn't see the audience. All we could do was just play our part. The lady from Atlanta was laughing, rolling and crying. They were taking her tissues and towels. She was falling over in the chair laughing and she couldn't be consoled.

After the play was over, the cast came out and sat on the side, so we could get our ratings from her. The church got quiet as she looked over to where we were sitting. She asked the question, *"Who is this Deacon Grey character?"* I raised my hand she said, *"That performance was outstanding. What acting school did you attend?"* I said I had never been to acting school. She then stated, *"It was amazing.'* Deacon Grey was birthed.

We had some major hit plays:

- Let's Just us Stay Friends
- Demon in My Bedroom
- There's Always Something Going On
- A Grey's Christmas Carol
- The Life and Times of Deacon Grey and many more.

I thought that would be the extent of it. Oh boy, was I wrong. People started calling me to come and do Comedy Skits and shows. Of course I did, for a price. The word got out like wildfire and now I was a traveling comedian. I was making extra money to make ends meet. OH MY GOD, was this real? I never advertised; it was just by word of mouth. My gift really did make room for me.

Acting taught me so many other things that helped develop my pulpit ministry. It helped me discern and gage audiences. It taught me timing and sync. It taught me call and response and how things flow to produce an end result. The next time I had to preach; it was life changing. The people saw the change in my delivery. It also brought me in sync with my leader.

The Lesson

Comedy has played a major part in me becoming the Second Man. Never despise the roads that God has designed to bring you to that expected end. As God begins to develop you, he will give you streams of income and your gift will bring you before great men. God is getting ready to monetize your gifts. You might be looking at one area of ministry, but God might be processing you in another area of ministry. You might arrive with a briefcase, a clergy collar and robe, but God will take the briefcase from you and give you a broom or he might give you a spoon to help in the kitchen.

Those are processing chambers. It is the broom that teaches you servitude and it's the spoon that teaches you hospitality and how to treat difficult people. Not only that, but it will also give you experience on how to deal with difficult situations. Hands on training is what you call it and that's the best training. Jesus was touched with the feeling or our infirmities and was at all points tempted. People can identify with you better when they know you have been where they have been.

> Wisdom comes from above; experience
> comes from going through and coming out.

Have you ever seen a second man act like he was the star? That's so annoying and the people can sense that. God is developing you to be the greatest support system your leader has because of your experience in all areas. A lot of times when people have problems, you won't even have to take them to your boss or leader you will be able to handle them yourself because of the process.

Not only do I get preaching engagements, I get calls to do comedy shows and plays. Can you believe that? It is another source of revenue just because I stepped back and occupied in my season of being disciplined.

As God was preparing me to be the second in command; there were certain lessons I had to learn. In order to learn those lessons, there were certain roads I had to take. Wisdom comes from above; experience comes from going through and coming out. Going through again and coming out again and learning from what you just came out of. God allowed me to work in every ministry in our church in order to give me the discernment that I needed to be in this great position. I wasn't seeking to be in all departments, but it just happened. In order for me to be processed through ministry, God had to remove me from the pulpit area of ministry and when that happened, He allowed me to work in other facets of ministry.

Just because you're being held back, doesn't mean you should leave and seek another job. It just means you're on hold for a season. There is a reason. Take some time and consider what's happening and where ever this space is carrying you. Just be mindful that there is a reason that you are there. Ask yourself the question, *"Why am I at this place at this particular time?" "What am I to learn while I'm here?" "What keys will I get to open up a greater door later?" "What concepts am I learning?"* Just realize that you are being empowered for another time and place and what you learn will be valuable later on. Stay the course. Chin up. The test will soon be over.

Chapter 12

MY TWO LIVING WIVES

The Story

The demands of ministry are great. It's just like a real marriage. Is it possible to have two living wives in our culture? When you make a vow, it is our responsibility to keep it as best we can. Until death do us part is the order of the day.

> "And the Lord God said, It is not good that the man should be alone; I will make him an help meet for him."
>
> *Genesis 2:18 KJV*

As the ceremony begins, the woman is draped in white, escorted to her future mate with music on point, romantic and moving. She proceeds to take her place on the stage beside her soon to be husband.

As the people watch, some with tears in their eyes, as the ceremony begins. Beloved, we are gathered here together to join this man and this woman in holy matrimony. If anyone objects to this union let him speak now or forever hold his peace. A hush goes over the audience. The front door of the church opens, another woman comes in dressed in white comes down the aisle and quietly sits down. All eyes on her, but she does not interfere with the wedding strangely enough. She comes to the reception and dances with the groom gives him a kiss and leaves. Nobody had a problem with it at that time. They thought she was just a guest.

As odd as it may sound this is exactly what happens when a man or woman marries a person in ministry, and let's go further than that, a person in business. There is a great responsibility for the person to cater to both relationships. The church is the other partner in the marriage. Now with Christ being in the center of the marriage, Christ being in the center of the church and Christ being in our lives, it seems like things should flow and be easier.

The wife in the marriage is emotional, needs attention, and loves to be worshipped by her husband. She requires his time, conversation, and she wants to be impregnated by him and have his children, and they live happily ever after.

Let's say the husband is a Pastor. He has another relationship going on, but it's not with another woman, but with his ministry. Let's take a look. The church needs attention. He gets calls all hours of the day and night that takes his attention. He has to be attentive to the needs of this ministry. Its demands are great. He spends late nights with her (ministry) and while his wife is calling he can't leave just yet because he's got 3 more appointments. The icing on the cake is the ministry is pregnant with purpose and destiny. He must balance himself between his wife and his ministry, and because the ministry is growing so fast it becomes infected and starts swelling. This takes more time to heal the infection, because if healing doesn't happen, death will occur. Then the leader is tossed to and fro, between the ministry and the wife.

The Lesson

Can you have a successful ministry and a failing marriage? It happens all the time. Can you have a great marriage and a failing ministry? Of Course. Can you have a great marriage and great ministry? Of course. Can you have a failing marriage and failing ministry. Yes. Can you have a failing marriage and great ministry? All of the above can happen.

(Your balancing act must be greater.)

There is a word called compartmentalization, where you don't mix things together. It's like a house. The bed doesn't belong in the kitchen. The toilet stool doesn't go in the living room. The stove doesn't go in the bedroom. Everything has its place. It is when you have a wife, family and then at the same time you have ministry/business that you don't bring your marriage to the ministry/business and you don't bring your ministry/business to the marriage. You keep everything in its place. If you are an assistant to the Man of God then your responsibility is greater, because you must not only attend to the ministry, you must also attend to him. Your balancing act must be greater.

Many attendants are losing their marriage and family because someone is being neglected and most of the time it's the wife. Now all the business at home is all over the church. The attendant and wife is fighting in parking lot at church and that shouldn't happen. At home, the attendant is demanding his wife to act and treat him with respect because Pastor says so. Now, he has the Pastor in the home; remember compartmentalization. The church should stay at church and the family issues should be home, and if that attendant is handling his business at home, he won't have to demand respect; he commands it. Balancing is key. I can't say this enough.

Chapter 13

MY REASONABLE SERVICE

The Story

People always want to be seen doing things. We have an announcement that on Tuesday night, we need the men to meet at the church to move chairs. Only 2 men will come to move 300- 500 chairs. Now, that service has started, the brothers will come up and ask, "*Can I help you?*" I'm saying to myself why are they asking now, I needed them the other night, but now I see.

All the Apostles and Bishops are here, the church is packed and now they are ready to put on a show, and a show it is. I watch them and chuckle because now they are embarrassing themselves. They are in front of all these people and don't know how to open up a chair. You have to remove the clip at the bottom. If they had come to help move chairs, then they would've known that, but I sit back a laugh and shake my head. Is that reasonable service?

Whenever I was with the Bishop, I would see things that nobody else saw. They would walk in with him in great conferences; I would stay back and clean out the truck or help at the book table, eat a bag of chips, sit back and watch. When he would finish preaching, I would be in the back with towels to dry him off, and make sure towels got to the cleaners. I would make sure he had new socks in the drawers, and I kept extra stuff in a suitcase in my car.

The guys that were serving him were always forgetting things and running all over the place because they never planned. I would just step in assist and leave. They would look at me and ask, *"What do you think you are doing? I got this."* I would say to them, *"It don't look like it."*

When I would go to Bishop's house, if I would see a room dirty, I would just go and put it order and come back to the meeting because he would always be teaching the boys and they would be at his feet. I didn't want to be at his feet. I saw those dishes were dirty, so I would go and wash the dishes.

Why were all these uncashed checks laying around? I would gather all the checks and would call the new church secretary and she told me to put them in the bank because he was not going to do it. I told Bishop I was going to deposit them, and there was money everywhere. Sometimes I'd be hanging up his suit and find wads of cash, thousands of dollars. I would give it to him or just lay it beside his bed.

I would drive him and notice the oil light on in his car. I would just go to his house and pick it up and have the oil changed. I noticed the guys that said, "*I got him.*", really didn't have him. They just had him when the crowd was present. There was so much work to be done, but very few people trying to do it.

I was never fond of being out front; I would always set things up and just sit back and watch things unfold. There was a price to pay to be out front and I'm not sure I was ready to pay that price. I wasn't ready for the hoopla that come along with it. Some people love it, but it brought on a whole lot of extra warfare and drama. People see you up front and because they see you with the Man or Woman of God, they figured you knew as much as they did. Then they would expect you to have answers to their problems.

A lot of times people would walk up to me, out of the blue and just start talking. They would go on and on and on until I would stop them and structure the conversation, so I could see where this is going or how I could fix it. All this rambling was torture to me. I like for people to get to the point as quickly as possible and let's fix this.

The Lesson

What is reasonable service? What does it look like? When does it show up and when does it end? It is written,

> *"I beseech you therefore, brethren, by the mercies of God, that ye present your bodies a living sacrifice, holy, acceptable unto God, which is your*
> *reasonable service." Romans 12:1 KJV*

I learned how to serve my leader by sitting back and watching from afar when nobody knew I was watching. I was the one least liked to be beside the Man of God. I wasn't that well educated in ministry ethics. As a leader, I wasn't eloquent in speech, but I just watched. I'm dangerous because I can figure anything out long as I watch. Every job that I had in my life I always ended up at the top. I have documentation to prove it. Everyone would come with problems, but I came with answers because I could always figure it out.

> My gift made room for me and brought me before great men.

I found my niche in the ministry and things began to expand. People opposed me, but it didn't work because I wasn't looking for a relaxing day. I wanted to work and if Bishop gave me an assignment, I wouldn't sleep at night because I was strategizing and planning. It's hard to whip a person who doesn't sleep, doesn't want any time off and who doesn't need to be seen. Amen!

My gift made room for me and brought me before great men. I couldn't preach as well as some of the guys that came through. I couldn't give as much as some of the guys. I couldn't prophesy or pray like some of the other guys, but nobody could beat me when it came to serving and this was my reasonable service.

Chapter 14

DUALITY

The Story

Many times, during my membership at Bethel I didn't think the Bishop liked me at all. It was obvious. It always seemed like he was always mad about something, either something that happened on the road, something that happened in the staff or something that happened in church. Something was always going on, meeting after meeting. Long hours were spent trying to get to the bottom of things.

I had the honor of serving two leaders in one. I served under the "Big Bloomer" and I served under the "Little Bloomer". It is written,

"No man can serve two masters: for either he will hate the one, and love the other; or else he will hold to the one, and despise the other. Ye cannot serve God and mammon." Matthew 6:24 KJV

I hated the Big Bloomer, but I loved the Little Bloomer.

When I was finally brought on as full time, I was brought on under the Little Bloomer. This one was a little less brutal or so I thought. It seems like after the sickness and other major events, he calmed down a little, but I was still traumatized by the experience of the Big Bloomer. A lot of the times things change in life, but we are still traumatized. We can't enjoy the benefits of the change even though the change is good.

I had always wanted to work in full time ministry, but I didn't know how it would work out. I saw the people who were currently employed, and they weren't making it. They were laughing at me, but I was a volunteer. I had a regular job. I saw that it wasn't easy working for Bishop. I thought at the all-night meetings, this one didn't like that one because he said this, they said that. There was so much childish behavior.

Growing with a ministry is a challenge, when I grew up in United Holy Church there were no meetings like this. People just said what they said. Take it or leave it. When God is developing a person for another level of service. The training can be brutal and combative. It's like boot camp. Boot camp isn't easy. The exercises are designed to get you in shape and prepare you for battle. The soldier that survives the battle took his training serious.

Lesson

Know that while you are in training to be a second or third man that God will allow you to see many facets of the individual that you are serving; you would have to. Even though your leader changed, certain aspects of his old character will still pop up from time to time. You will have to be ready to deal with them accordingly.

You should be able to detect vibrations when you are in the presence of your leader. I can tell if Bishop is agitated. He doesn't have to say a word. I don't say anything. I just do my job until he finally says something, because me speaking would further agitate the situation. Sometimes I would end up leaving and he would call on the phone when he was ready to talk and tell me why he was agitated.

I'm a calm person, things don't bother me. I have a way of processing things and I don't know how it happens, but it does. I never had a problem with anger because of the way I think. I don't know whether it's good or bad, that's just how it is. I try not to let people know what my triggers are. I could be upset, but unless I mentioned it, you wouldn't know. If you are assigned to a great leader, make sure you have a calming effect on him or her because he is dealing with a lot of problems at once and you don't want to add to the equation.

I love the Bloomer that I'm serving now. I'm older and my nerves can't handle a whole lot of drama now. When a tree is tender, it can be trained and can sway with the wind but when a tree gets old it's solid, can't be trained and limbs break and crash on houses and can cause great damage.

(Get focused and become the pillar that you are.)

We all have choices and many times we must live with the choices that we make. Sad to say most times we make wrong choices and end up paying the consequences. If you are reading this book as a person that's aspiring to assist a great leader whether spiritual or secular and, you desire to serve for any length of time, then you will see your leader change right before your eyes. What causes these changes? Sometimes life circumstances change i.e., your leader may get a divorce or someone in his life might transition. Remember your mentor or leader is a real person who has an assignment on his life. The pressure will be 10 times greater than the average person just because of the demands.

As the leader grows and matures, you as an assistant will have to do the same. Sad as it may be, some leaders don't get better some will get worse and if you are committed to him or her, you will stick with them. It is written,

"And let us not be weary in well doing: for in due season we shall reap, if we faint not."

Galatians 6:9 KJV

Most assistants are not stable themselves. How can you assist a major player in life if you're not stable? How can you assist in financial matters if yours are not in order? How can you clean his house if you can't clean your own house? How can you deal with their family correctly if you don't know how to deal with your family? It's a lot to process, but if you going to take this on you have to get focused and become the pillar that you are.

The Drill Sergeant has an assignment and that is not to be a friend of the soldier, but to make him tough and to make him believe he can take a bullet. Make him believe he can run through a wall.

Training is not easy, and it never was meant to be. If you are in training, by God, to assist a General then you know your training has to be intense. To just jump up and run to another ministry is disobedient and childish, you will never fulfill your purpose if you always on the run. It's time to take it like a man or woman and if you do that you will be an honorable soldier.

Chapter 15

DID I ASK YOU THAT?

The Story

Bishop has taught me many valuable lessons over the years. Many lessons I will never forget. He would ask me a question and I wouldn't answer the question. I would just go on rambling on and on and on and he would stop me and say, "*You didn't answer the question.*" I would say I did, but no I didn't answer that exact question, but I answered it in the way I thought it should be answered, well he said emphatically, "*We going to jail.*" What did he mean by that? Bishop said, "*If we were to go to court, they put you on the stand, ask you a question and you just go on and on, then we going to jail. Never over answer the question just answer what I ask you.*" That takes discipline especially when all your life you are used to just rambling off at the mouth without anyone holding you accountable.

Businessmen will never trust you in meetings because you will reveal all the secrets in one answer.

Bishop would ask me a question like, *"How many people are in the sanctuary?"* And I would answer, *"There are about 100 people in the sanctuary but another 20 cars just pulled up and there are 10 people in the lobby?"* He would stop me and say, *"I didn't ask you all of that. Answer the question."* How many times do we end up telling our leader's business even though we didn't mean to, but the damage is already done? You have got to have someone in your corner to always check you and polish you for your next level or nobody will be able to trust you with secrets. Then I understood. I have to catch myself, when someone ask me a question. It is written,

> *"But let your communication be, Yea, yea; Nay, nay: for whatsoever is more than these cometh of evil."*
>
> *Matthew 5:37 KJV*

Lesson

Learning how to be a leader or being an assistant is not easy especially when you're used to doing things a certain way. Have you ever listened to people talk and see how people communicate? You really don't notice it until you are challenged to communicate better. For example, I was listening to a conversation where two old ladies were conversing. One lady asked the other lady where she was going and the lady responded, "Well, I was going to the grocery store, but I was waiting for my daughter to pick me up, but she was running late. I told her to make sure she was on time because I had to get back home to cook dinner for my grandkids. My grandson had just got out of prison. You know he did some drugs and the police came to the house and took him, so I had to put the house up to bond him out of jail."

> Being in leadership requires you to be sharp.

When I heard that conversation, I said, "Oh my God, do I sound like that?" All the lady asked her was, where was she going. Can you imagine all the extra information that lady gave? That kind of talk would uncover a lot of secrets and if you are in business, you can't afford to have people around you that reveal too much information. It will allow your competitors to see inside your business.

It's hard to teach an old dog new tricks. You have to show him old tricks in a new way. Being in leadership requires you to be sharp. Always on your toes. Always thinking. Always watching. Seeing things that are not obvious and hearing things that nobody else can hear. Is that easy? No. You have to think outside the box. You have to think on a larger scale, unless you just want to lead in mediocrity. Why stop at mediocrity? Go to greatness. Be an overachiever. For He has made us more than conquerors, not just a conqueror, but more than conqueror. There are higher heights and deeper debts.

> *"I press toward the mark for the prize of the high calling of God in Christ Jesus."*
>
> *Philippians 3:14 KJV*

Being a leader, you have to determine what to say and when to say it. That's not easy. What you say influences people's lives and can set them on a course of victory or defeat. That is a great undertaking. Some people have nerve to say, "*Speak your mind.*" Is that a good thing? If you speak your mind, then what's in there will come out.

Chapter 16

CHEAPSKATE

The Story

B ishop Bloomer is a very successful businessman in the secular as well as in the gospel arena. He could only be as great as the team around him. He is not able to personally touch or communicate with his public, but also has a supporting team that holds his hands up and keeps the engine running. As the team is in the background, they have to understand that he got where he is by sowing and sowing and sowing. You can't be stingy and a sower at the same time. You will cling to the one and despise the other.

Many times Bishop stands up and commands offering of thousands of dollars. The assistants must also learn that principal of sowing, reaping, and command. In order to command that kind of money, there must be respect. The people have to respect you. When the people are giving, even though they are giving to God, you are the one receiving it. They are putting it in your hand. The attendants must be seen as giving. You don't give to be seen, but you must be seen giving. Being a cheapskate won't cut it this time around.

For many years, money was an issue for me. It was a struggle just to survive day by day. I didn't feel like I was that smart, at least that was what I was told. I succumbed to the voices of the people around me. Most jobs that I had, I got through temp services, and because I was a hard worker, came to work every day, they kept me on. I would grow with the company, but grow where there was always a ceiling. You know what that means. There's no growth. All you look forward to was a paycheck and possibly a bonus at the end of the year that would consist of maybe six hundred dollars.

I got locked into a mindset of mediocrity. When you have a leader, who is constantly telling you that you have the ability to do more and not to settle for less, it stretches you. Stretching becomes uncomfortable. If you want to get out of the everyday mundane life, you have to be challenged. When you are thirty five years old and forty years old, who wants another man in your face telling you to grow up? That's what happened to me.

Those of you that can remember the television show Gomer Pyle back in the seventies and 80's, that is exactly what I'm talking about. A somewhat mean Sergeant yelling and screaming in the face of a somewhat shy private. Without the constant badgering of the Sergeant, Gomer would have never been transformed into the statesman that he became. The key is to stick with it and stay the course. Use the insults as fuel for progress. Don't allow yourself to become a quitter and don't allow yourself to become intimidated or offended. Make it an opportunity to become a statesman.

The Lesson

When it came to money, I had to be challenged, and that's what caused me to grow financially. There is a language to money and only those who understand it will benefit from it. If you are assisting your leader and he has to receive an offering or even give a seminar on money, would you be able to assist him and be confident and fluent so that you can command an offering or generate finances to the point that if he is absent, you're able to carry out the assignment and the budget is met as if he was there? If not, then nothing is learned from him mentoring you. Do you understand the principle of a seed? What do you do when you sow a seed and the seed then dies before it is resurrected to become a harvest? Do you understand the principles of tithing and sacrifices? One opens up the heavens and the other one can cause blessings and opens you up. Nobody wants to follow a broke leader because the anointing flows from the head down, and assistants are part of that flow.

> There is always a lesson to be learned especially when it comes to finances.

If a leader has his finances in order then he should want his assistant's finances in order. There must be money conversations. Money conversations are very uncomfortable especially when you don't want to be held accountable for your spending. A lot of the times only the leader is financially secure.

There is always a lesson to be learned when dealing with a Leader, General or Mentor especially when it comes to finances. Why learn a lesson when all you have to do is give me the money? A lot of people like to hang around because of the benefits of being with the leader such as, the shopping trips, the restaurants, the free flights in the private jets, and the automobiles. That's a great incentive to serve the leader. What if all of that doesn't come? After all it's not yours, right? What if the riches that you are to receive is wisdom that comes from the lips of your leader that you are serving.

Wisdom will take you so much further than money. In fact, it's the wisdom that brings the ideas that causes money to come. It is written,

"Wisdom is the principal thing; therefore get wisdom: and with all thy getting get understanding." Proverbs 4:7 KJV

In all thy getting, get an understanding on how money operates. Money has wings. It will fly away. It has emotions; it will shut down on you. Money has ears; it can hear you calling. It has feet; it can come to you, or it can leave.

Learning a lesson on money will greatly impact your life. You will be able to assist your leader at a greater level. When he tells you to wash his car or put a suit in the cleaners, you won't have to ask for 20 dollars, you just go and do it. You don't get lessons about money from a broke person. What can they tell you? In fact, they don't even know the linguistics of money. All the attendants are clones of the leader. Everyone should have their own identity with a hint of their leader's traits on them. It's a great honor for any leader to see his mentees stand up and publicly support the cause.

Chapter 17

THEY DIDN'T SEE ME COMING

The Story

Unassuming, quiet, timid, not that smart, broke, so they thought that was who I was. How does a person like that end up being the Second Man in charge? Can you explain that? The art of warfare is deception. You never show your hand and you never let the enemy see you coming. The problem that most people have is that they announce who they are, and it gives the enemy ammunition to destroy you.

My plan is different, when I arrive nobody suspects anything because I don't look threatening. The opponent relaxes around me and tells me their secrets. What can a country guy from Goldsboro do? That's what I want them to believe. When all the while I'm taking notes because when I come back I'm taking over.

That has happened on all my jobs. I always ended on top and the ones who were determined to get there told me their strategy and I used it to my advantage. Keep your mouth closed, and don't let the devil or component see you coming.

The brothers had a men's retreat in Pinehurst, NC. There were about 100 brothers present and we were waiting in anticipation for Bishop to come and impart unto us. When Bishop mounted the podium, he asked everyone what their goals were, and we all had to give out short- and long-term goals. Many of the brothers were saying that they were going to be businessmen, or investors. Some stated that they were going to flip houses or maybe own a car lot. Oh my God! Their goals were so intimidating to me because I didn't have plans like that. When they got to me all I said was I'm going to be faithful in ministry and reap the benefits. When I said that, I heard people snickering in the room as if what I said was funny, but I knew what I wanted to do.

It's sad to say many of those brothers are in jail, some are back on drugs, some are barely making it, and all but 2 out of 100 men have moved on. When they come back and want to meet with Bishop, they have to come through me. How did that happen? You never judge a man by his outward appearance. Those who appear most strong are the weakest and those who appear most weakest are the strongest. Let the weak say I'm strong, let the poor say I'm rich.

The Lesson

Being looked over is not fun especially when you know what's going on. God knows what's going on and he is the one who orchestrated it. The scripture says,

God has to deal with character flaws in the individual that would hinder him or her later on.

"And he said unto me, My grace is sufficient for thee: for my strength is made perfect in weakness.
Most gladly therefore will I rather glory in my infirmities, that the power of Christ may rest upon me."

2 Corinthians 12:9 KJV

Whenever you are looked over and or picked on, a majority of the time it's God showing His strength in the face of people who are flexing their own strength and we know who wins in the end.

In developing a Second Man, God has to deal with character flaws in the individual that would hinder him or her later on. For example, if the person is weak and timid, God would have to build strength in this person. How would he do it? By challenging those areas through hardness, and over a period, the weak person will start standing up for himself.

You can't assist a general and be weak and passive. You have to be assertive and confrontational. You must be in command, confident, and authoritative. It takes time to develop these characteristics, but if you endure the storm, the test and the rejection, God will reward you with the Keys to the Kingdom. It's the Keys that give you the authority and access. The scripture says,

> *"But as many as received him, to them gave he power to become the sons of God, even to them that believe on his name:" John 1:12 KJV*

If God has greatness in store for you, you don't have to announce it. Just keep your same posture, and watch things manifest just like God said. Don't be intimidated by people who don't know where you are going. Pay no attention to naysayers don't even respond to them at all. It's a waste of time trying to defend yourself. Let God do it, then you will be able to look back and see how God has developed you into a vessel of honor and placed you in the mansion with the best China. I am unassuming, shy, laidback and not that smart, but I'm here.

Chapter 18

THE WIND DON'T BLOW LIKE THAT FOR US

The Story

I would love for Bishop to tell me things in advance, so I can have time to navigate and give him the best service. That would be awesome to me, if he would just give me a week or twos notice and not wait until the last minute to do something. It's seems like it never happened that way. He always calls 3 minutes before he goes in the pulpit and always needs 10 scriptures and definitions and props for an illustrated sermon. Wherever I'm at, I have to stop what I'm doing, whether it's on a date or shopping in the mall, driving down a busy highway or even at a family reunion, when duty calls, I must go.

Sometimes it's so frustrating because if I knew in advance that he would need this I would have been better prepared. It couldn't be that easy.

Always rushing...always in a hurry... always now, now, now. Doesn't he understand I have a life too?

One day, I was jogging on a 3 mile trail in the woods. My car was 2 miles behind me and I was enjoying a sunny day. Bishop called and said he needed to send money to a needy family and they needed it right away. In fact, he said they were already at the Western Union waiting for it and he stated that they hadn't eaten. Well, that's not my problem I was enjoying my day, so I told him I would get the money to them quickly. The he went on to say, *"The King's business required haste."* Ok Bishop, but I'm 2 miles away from my car and I'm tired so that means it would take me at least an hour to get back to my car and get to the bank and go to a Western Union. He hung up. Now I'm going to finish my hike then I'm going to Western Union.
He wouldn't know I hadn't left yet.

Nooooo! He called me every five minutes and kept asking, " *Are you there yet? Are you there yet? Are you there yet?"* I'm cutting this phone off, if he calls me one more time. Finally, I just turn around and run back to my car. An afternoon of leisure turns into a frantic rush to take someone some money. Now it hit me, they weren't at the Western Union. He just said that to get me to rush, because when I called them to give them the reference number it sounded like they were half sleep. I wasted an afternoon of leisure and didn't have to. I made up for it later.

Lack of planning on their part doesn't constitute an emergency on my part. I got tired of all this rushing and last-minute assignments. I was going to confront Bishop about this, and tell him how I could do a better job, if I had advance notice.

He calls me one day and I figured that was the right time to let him have it. I said Bishop you need to start considering where I'm at and what I'm doing when you call me because a lot of times when you call I'm driving or taking care of business, or doing the food giveaway and I'm extremely busy, so you need to consider that. There, I said it and got it out of my system. I felt better now what his response going to be. He proceeded to say, "*This conversation is necessary. Listen to me. We have a warfare ministry and can't always tell when or where the wind is blowing. We just got to be ready to move with the wind. Sometimes I don't know what I am gonna do, and if I don't know, then how can I tell you. The wind doesn't blow like that for us."* I knew what that meant without even asking. Always be prepared to get the assignment done.

The Lesson

Our Pastor, President, CEO or whoever the first man is, sometimes it seems like they don't understand our point of view. Are they supposed to? Are they called to understand us or are we called to understand them, or all of the above? It's a relationship. In order to be in a relationship, you have to be able to relate to one another. There must be some kind of understanding. You have to understand your leader in order to serve him.

(You have an assignment to know everything you have to know that would help you serve him.)

You understand him by paying close attention to details. That means you have to key in on what's obvious and not obvious. You can be in two separate locations and can pinpoint what he is doing without even asking him, because you study his patterns when you are with him. I'm with Bishop so much that I can tell when he's sleep, when he's on the phone and when he's watching television. It's like a marriage when the two become one, that's if your called to that person. If you are called, then you have an assignment to know everything you have to know that would help you serve him. I know how Bishop pay his bills, or if he even wants to pay that bill at that moment. It's called paying attention to the details.

Chapter 19

Y'ALL STOP RUNNING AROUND, I GOT THIS

The Story

As the Second Man, sometimes you are put in a position of making decisions and judging situations before it gets to your leader. What do you do when you're in a position to do something for others, but don't want it to look like it's you doing it. For example, what if you see potential in someone and you know it's an area that much needed, but because of their positioning they wouldn't be noticed? You have to be clever and situate that person in a way that you know they will be noticed.

There was a situation in the ministry where we needed a position filled and because of my many duties at the time and lack of experience, I wouldn't be able to fill it. I knew just the person who could handle it. Ironically, years before Bishop had spoken into this person's life and he had forgotten he had spoken it. The opportunity came as we had a discussion of who would fill that position. When I mentioned the name he asked, "Do you think she can get the job done?" I said, "Of course and the person took the position and has become an asset to the ministry.

The person didn't know she was being considered. I knew because of working with her previously, that she was capable of such a task. As a Second Man there are things you take note of when you're moving among the people. If your leader is sharp and can see certainly you must have that same quality and should be able to judge accordingly.

There is an art to serving a man like Bishop Bloomer and if you are serving a General or a highprofile person you must not only be anointed, you must also be knowledgeable in many facets of life because of the business that he does spiritually and secularly. For example, if a member needs a car and comes to Bishop and he has the heart to give it to them, it's the assistant job to find the car. Bishop doesn't have time to go car hunting. What if a person in our overseas ministry in Africa needs emergency financial help? It's the assistant's job to make sure that the ministries can get the transaction done. Let's say someone dies in the church and doesn't have knowledge of what the next step is, it's the assistant's job to have the connections that are needed to fulfill their need. The list goes on and on.

There is more to this than carrying a briefcase and keys to his Mercedes. How well does the assistant know the scriptures? If Bishop is a scripture man and you are his assistant you also must have a strong scripture base. 99.9% of the time, I help Bishop prepare sermons by looking up scriptures, definitions, looking for items for illustrated sermons and etc.

One of Bishop's Power Principles that has taught us over the years is, *"If you don't see it before you see it, when it manifests you won't recognize it."* You have to see the problem before it happens, I know what potential problems that Bishop is going to have. He is going to lose his keys, that's a fact. I always have a spare with me. He is going to get locked out, so I keep an extra house key. He is going to lose his glasses, so I keep 5 extra pair within my reach. Sometimes he forgets his passwords, so I know all of them in case he calls; the list goes on. I've been with him long enough to know these things. In fact, I can't remember my passwords and social security numbers, but I remember his. I have come home and my lights are out because I forgot to pay my light bill. I have to make sure he is ok.

A lot of the time when Bishop gets to church, the attendants are looking for things. They call me and I tell them, *"Relax I got this. I will be there in five minutes."* One year, we were flying into Florida and Bishop wanted to do an illustration sermon. We landed at about 5:00pm and Service started at 7:00pm. He gave me a list of about 20 items I needed to pull together for the service. I had to find a Walmart, an arts and craft store, dollar store, pick up these items, bring them to the hotel, assemble them and pack them for service. Then I had to go get Bishop something to eat, get his clothes out of the suitcase and get them ready. I had to go back to the room to get my clothes ready, call the driver of the ministry and find out his location, and get dressed. Next, I had to go wake Bishop up, and help him get ready and at the same time, Bishop wants me to give him a message title for that night. First of all, my mind is all over the place. I can't focus on a title. "Ain't he the preacher?" is what I'm thinking to myself.

Now my phone rings and we have an emergency back home at the church that needs my attention. I can't tell him right now because he has to preach to 3000 people, so I have to step out in the lobby of hotel and fix that situation. At the same time, my family is having an emergency. Now, Bishop is ringing my phone off the hook, but I can't switch over because I'm on phone with the county jail getting a close family member a bondsman. When I get back to Bishop's room, he talks to me about staying focused. How can you focus when you handling 10 things at once and all these things require your immediate attention? Somehow, I manage to handle it. The driver arrives and we load up and head for service.

Lesson

What a task it is to make sure everything thing is in place. I had to learn to think ahead to fix a problem before it happens. In the type of ministry that we have there are always problems, but if you can see it before you see it, when the problem comes, it's already solved. That means you have to always be thinking of what could possibly go wrong. When it goes wrong, everyone else is panicking, but I solved it weeks ago in my mind. When they come to me, I just give them the solution and the day is saved and we're able to move on.

(If you're attending to a general or great man, always have things handy, within reach.)

Always be prepared for the unexpected. At any given time day or night Bishop might call and need bank wire information and need it in five minutes. There's no time to run back home or call a secretary, I have got to have it at my fingertips. If you're attending to a general or great man, always have things handy, within reach, then you will be able to assist him and not frustrate him, because when he is frustrated he is not at his best,

Chapter 20

STOP! SIT DOWN SERVANT

The Story

During the course of my training as Second Man, I didn't know I was in training as Second Man. I was openly rebuked 3 times and was told to sit down, so what did I do? I went a sat down. Was I bothered? Yes. Did I consider leaving? Yes, but I went over to my seat and sat down. I thought to myself, I was tired anyway, let those other people do something, because I knew they would be calling me back because these men are lazy.

I sat down and got a grip on things until it was time for the tent revival. They needed someone to oversee it and here was the time God was setting me back up. Stop all this running from place to place, go somewhere and sit your happy self down. Get a strategy plan and watch God breathe on it and he will take you to levels unknown.

One of my favorite old songs I like to sing is, "Sit down servant, sit down, sit down and rest a little while. I didn't know that in my life I was going to experience a sit down. Many times while God is molding and shaping you into a vessel of honor, he has to crack the whip on you. The scripture says,

> *"Thou therefore endure hardness, as a good soldier of Jesus Christ."*
>
> *2 Timothy 2:3 KJV*

To read it is one thing, but to experience it is another thing. I thought going to the top would be peaches and crème, but then I realized I had to eat garlic and onions.

The Lesson

When I travel and watch how other assistants treat their leaders sometimes, I say to myself, "*I need just a few days with them to teach them some things.*" Many of them are too sensitive and wear their heart on their shoulders. You should know your leader inside and out and to know not to take it personally. That's a process and has to be learned through experience. It can't be taught overnight.

(Running is not the solution.)

Being with Bishop, I have learned not to get embarrassed easily because anything is liable to come out of his mouth and I have to be prepared. Most assistants keep an exit strategy. When things get tough they say, *"I'm outta here,"* and off to the next ministry they go. When they get there, they have to encounter the same test that they ran from in the former ministry. Running is not the solution. Well, you might say God didn't send me here. I'm going where God wants me. First of all, you don't know the voice of God. If you did. you would know that running is not the solution. If God was leading you to run, then why when you arrive, you have to start manipulating to get positions. The scripture says,

"Be still, and know that I am God: I will be exalted among the heathen, I will be exalted in the earth."

Psalm 46:10 KJV

Sometimes God trains us in places in which we are not comfortable. If you run, you won't get the lesson, and if God didn't send you there, He gave you the grace to stay there long enough to glean on what to do and what not to do so stand still.

You might say you are a Prophet, and your Mentor doesn't believe in prophetic. It's not your job to convince him or her, but it's your job to serve and keep your big prophetic mouth closed and grow and realize it's not your time at this moment; it's his time. How do you handle open rebuke? Do you run or do you stay? Do you lash back or do you sit back and regroup?

Chapter 21

I HAVE A LIFE TOO

The Story

I had a conversation with Bishop this morning, which so happened to be a Thursday. Bishop always says the Lord speaks to him on Thursday's and seeing that I have been with him for over 26 years, I know that to be true. He was talking about First Man and Second Man positions in an organization, business, or ministry.

He began to share with me about when the ministry first started he was a Second Man in a First Man's position, and I was a Second Man in a Second Man's position. Wait a minute. We have a problem. If he is the Second Man and I am the Second Man, then I see where the conflict was. We were both in the same position.

I wasn't trying to take his position. I didn't want it, doesn't he know that? I guess he didn't. I remember because when we were in conflict he would always say this is my ministry. Well, no one was challenging that, why did he feel that way? 20 years later I fully understand, after we had our talk. Wow, it's clear to me now.

We both were in the same position and we were fighting for our space. We were in competition with one another, and it had to be his way. I had no problem with that, he was the Pastor. He was still the Second Man, but that's what I was. All I wanted to do was put up a tent, help drive the van, direct the choir, clean the building and just serve. How was I a threat? I didn't want the headache of trying be Pastor. He was Pastor and he was the Second Man, and I'm sure we were intimidating each other in that position.

Recently, I noticed that we are not in conflict any more. What happened? Bishop finally realized it and left being the Second Man and started being the First Man and he allowed me to be the Second Man. Now my eyes are open.

The Lesson

What do you do when you're serving a leader and just doing your job and you find out that your leader hasn't moved up as in the case of Elijah and Elisha? Elisha couldn't occupy until Elijah got caught up to be able to get the double portion. If you're the Second Man in a ministry or organization, what is it that is expected of you? When you make decisions, what are those decisions based on? How do you know when you're making the right decisions or should you be making decisions at all?

> You command respect by letting your yea be yea, your nay be nay, by meaning what you say, and not becoming too familiar with the people.

In order to be a Second Man, there must be a level of trust from the First Man. However, if the ministry is new and there has been no history, how can there be trust? How do you build trust? In order for trust to be established, there must be respect and respect must be commanded not demanded. How do you command respect? You command respect by letting your yea be yea, your nay be nay, by meaning what you say, and not becoming too familiar with the people.

The old folks used to say, *"If you play with the dog, he will lick you in the face,"* and that's a true proverb. Always remember it is the First Man that has the vision, the insight and the marching orders. Anything with two heads is a freak. You have to know the role that you play being the Second Man.

Let's talk about some problems that we incur as being the Second Man. When a Second Man is in position and a problem arises, the first thought that comes to mind is what Jesus would do. That's politically correct, but not in the sense of you being a Second Man. The first thought should be what would my Pastor do in this situation, and if you are in sync with your Pastor then you would know exactly what he would do.

Many times, I can finish Bishop's sentence because I've been with him for so long. I know what he is thinking. It just happens, but it took years of mistakes and rebukes to get to that point. We come from two different walks of life. It was hard at first because I was considered the nice guy and Bishop was the hard stern guy. I would make decisions based on my kindness and was missing the real picture. Bishop would always see the big picture and would point it out to me and show me where I missed it.

It took years of trial and error until eventually I clocked him. Bishop has experience and discernment that I didn't have because of where he has been. He traveled all over the world many times over and I had never been out of North Carolina, outside the county line. If that was the case, I should have spent more time listening than talking. Oftentimes, we are running our mouth and miss the impartation. Don't be a know it all, but be a see it all and hear it all.

Bishop would often say to me, *"You got to see things before it happen in order to be a good leader."* Well, how do you do that? First, you have to have a prayer life because prayer gives you the jump on things. I did have a prayer life, but why was I still missing so many things? The problem was I was praying prayers and not talking to God. Wow really? I pray at least an hour a day and wasn't talking to God. Right, I was praying traditional prayers and was getting nowhere. I was on my knees for an hour my eyes were closed, but I was getting nowhere.

When I found out prayer was basically communicating with God then I realized I was doing it all wrong. I now found out that prayer was like breathing. Men should always pray and not faint.

Now it is possible to think prayers, sing prayers and now God talks back to me. He shows me things, gives me insight and in His own way giving me the jump on things. Now when problems arise, I already have the solution because I was in tune with my leader and in tune with God. This is amazing. No more meetings about how I missed things. Praise the Lord! God is really developing me into a Second Man. Remember as the Second Man, it's not our job to hear from God, but it's our job to hear from the First Man.

Chapter 22

THE MIDAS TOUCH

The Story

We serve cookies and we had a new lady on the were having an event and Bishop wanted to hospitality team. Everyone else had left. The lady proceeded to get the cookies and wrapped each cookie in aluminum foil and was headed to the sanctuary. We were seated in the back, as we noticed this beginning to unfold, we ran over to the lady and told her that was not the way to serve cookies. We took each cookie and placed them in a small decorative cookie zip lock bag which was more professional. That was the small Midas touch that was needed to ensure the integrity of the meeting was kept intact. The Midas touch will pack an event out. Clean bathrooms, every chair in sync with the decor of the room, color coordination is on point, everything centered to the room, and everyone in uniform, and etc. are all part of the Midas touch.

I sit and watch a lot of services online and I just laugh because the Pastor is very gifted and anointed and could possibly be world renown at the click of a few buttons, but how he is packaged is shameful. The people sitting behind him are chewing gum and talking. While he is proving his point, I look at the stained glass window behind him and it is dusty you can see cobwebs in the corner. Someone in the choir behind him is holding a baby who is agitated and keeps crying during his presentation, but nobody notices these things and then they wonder why no one comes to his services. What is the missing element and why can no one can point these things out?

Many times, Bishop and I will be engaged in a project. A lot of times we will be pressed for time, and I have to move to my next assignment. That caused me to do a rush job and it would be ok, but not the best. Bishop will see it and start talking about the Midas touch. What is the Midas touch? In mythology, it's the ability to turn everything into gold. It's that extra touch that brings out the splendor in a product.

Lesson

You want to be close to your leader? Most people believe that if they touch the leader that the anointing will fall off of the leader and fall on them just like that. No prayer. No sacrifice. No consecration. Just rub your hand on my shoulder and shazam, there it is. Oh really? Are you in Lala land? Why do you want to be close to your leader? Is it just for the fame and popularity that comes with the position? Is it just to hear your name called and sit in the uppermost seat at services and meetings? Let's be honest, that's what people are looking for, recognition and acceptance, but it goes far beyond that. It goes so much further.

There is more work to be done behind the scenes than is done in the spotlight. A lot of times people just throw things together just for the sake of saying you're working for the Lord. Is that the way you're supposed to do it? Will God accept anything? You won't take a cheeseburger from McDonald's like that. It must be well presented.

> If he can't trust you to do a flyer, something
> as simple as that, how can he trust you to
> represent the people to him?

A lot of leaders or leader assistants don't have that Midas touch. That's why they are not at the top of their game. For example, your leader or First Man has an event and has invited thousands of people. In order to get the people to come, there must be advertising. Someone has the responsibility to do the flyers. When the flyers are finished, they just pass them out. No one takes the time to really critique the flyer to make sure the colors are popping. After all, who reads a dull flyer? As you begin to read it, a couple words are spelled wrong, but that's ok send it any way. Noooooooooo! Why would you send a flyer to businessmen, lawyer, judges, investors that's not 100 percent flawless? They will say, if you handle your business like that then you will handle them like that. You will end up with a substandard crowd, but the target crowd was turned off by the flyer.

As the Second Man, you have to make sure it's flawless before you present it to the First Man or your leader, because it says a lot about you and your ability to judge matters. If he can't trust you to do a flyer, something as simple as that, how can he trust you to represent the people to him?

Chapter 23

GETTING IN THE WAY OF WHAT I'M FEELING

The Story

There is an open mic service and people are asked to come to the mic and ask questions. Who is the first person to the mic? The woman with the vision who is not allowed to see the Pastor. She goes on to say she desires a meeting with the Pastor and can't get through and the Pastor asks, *"Who did you talk to?"* And she says, *"Your assistant. I have important issue I'm dealing with I need counseling."* The Pastor says, *"Well, I don't have private meetings with women. There has to be someone present."* She hesitates, and states that she doesn't want anyone knowing her business. The assistant knows what her motive is so he informs security. A meeting is scheduled and when the woman finally gets a meeting, she tells the Pastor that she likes him. Now the Pastor asks his assistant, *"How did she get past the gate? Something should have been said because this woman could say anything and start a scandal."*

Bishop has a program called Warfarecology that causes him to be on live every day. We had a situation where a lady inboxed him and said she was disappointed with him. As I continued to read, she went on to say that Bishop had promised to look out for her and they were to communicate daily but he didn't keep his end of the bargain. What! Omg! She said she sowed in the ministry and he didn't appreciate it. She stated that she was leaving the church. Something was terribly wrong.

I called this woman to find out what the situation was all about. She stated that she talked to Bishop on Facebook and he made all of these promises to her. I said what!!!! To make a long story short, I had to tell her, Bishop isn't on Social Media. He doesn't talk to anyone online. Bishop doesn't know how to use Social Media. He has a team that handles that. She then went on to say that Bishop was coming on to her. I knew that was a lie because Bishop has a certain type. She has to be young, petite, a hint of ugly, and if he was interested I would be the one to set it up. Who were you talking to? Come to find out she was talking to a fake profile. Bishop tells them that all the time that he is not on Social Media, but this was feeding into her fantasy and she went along with it. She then understood and got delivered at the moment.

It's cases like this all the time. We have women sending huge Valentine's cards to the church via Fedex. It was so big I couldn't get the card in the car. We had woman to try and put a spell on panties and put them in the flowerpot at the altar. They text my phone at 4:00am stating they love him. They tell me their dreams and visions hoping I would tell Bishop. It's been like this for 30 years and we have to do interference so everyone is covered because these women love God and they also love Bishop. The scripture tells us,

"Now we exhort you, brethren, warn them that are unruly, comfort the feebleminded, support the weak, be patient toward all men."

1 Thessalonians 5:14

That's another part of our ministry, to make sure no soul is lost.

The Lesson

This happens all the time people plotting to fulfill their fantasy with the Pastor. The people who are in charge of protecting the Pastors must be on their guard because many people are targeting them and befriend them just so they can get close to Pastor. You better know it. Remember it's not about you and don't you forget it. In fact, if you think it's about you, try your luck, pull out, leave and see how many people will follow you. Don't be deceived.

(Remember it's not about you and don't you forget it.)

It's about the anointing that rests upon your man or woman of God that attracts people to them and people become infatuated with the person and fall in love with an idea or fantasy. Let's be real, if they only knew being involved with a Pastor is a lonely life because you have to share him with the church the community the world. I'm sure they never thought about that. All they want to do is wear the big hats and dress in St. John knits. Well my sister, all you're going to have is a dress and a hat, but you will wear it home alone because he got three meetings scheduled. Did your fantasy show you that?

Being a Second Man will make you popular and this is not just talking about the men. You might have a woman in charge and have to assist her. It does not matter the gender, the lesson is still the same. Being in leadership gives you a special appeal, you can be ugly as sin, but if you get anointed it will make you fine as wine. This is a mystery, but that's the way it is. Many women don't have the secret formula to getting in touch with the Pastor. They admire him or her from a distance, but man oh man some women are ready for the challenge. They come with the mindset, I want him and I'm going to get him by any means necessary.

They scope out and see who is the closest one to the leader low and behold it's the Second Man. He needs an intercessor. She goes on to say, *"I'm going to tell the Second Man, I'm praying (preying) for him and Pastor."* That's how it all get started over prayer (or a preyer).

This woman is clever because she is spiritual. She has a dream and has to share it with the Pastor, but the Second Man won't allow it. She is insisting and adamant about sharing her vision, but without much success. The battle begins.

The Second Man has to manage these women with these crazy ideas in their heads. They are angry and mad, and because the Second Man has got to manage, so many things he has her number in his phone. She is on the prayer group.

Many nights at 4:00am, text messages will come through my phone stating that they love the Pastor, miss him and send him this message. I respond and say, *"Please don't do this; Pastor doesn't want you. We don't want you to leave the ministry, but you must control yourself or I will take away your access to me."* Many of them apologize and start searching other ways to reach him like by writing letter and sending it. I see those also. It's our job to protect the leader, to be on guard. Stay alert because your adversary, the devil, is as a roaring lion is seeking whom he may devour. If the Second Man is not sharp, the roaring lion will devour and destroy. So stay alert, your leader is depending on you.

LOYALTY IS THE NEW CASH

All through life we strive to be successful. We work 9-5 hoping for a big payday. We find prophets or someone to speak into our financial future. We go to motivational seminars to get motivated to be successful. Let's sell insurance, let's invest in crypto currency, or better yet why don't you buy from yourself. So many schemes until your friends hate to see you coming because, "Papa always got a new bag," every week it's something different. Let's try this Pyramid or that pyramid so we can tap into these 10 steps to being a Millionaire. It all sounds wonderful, but what if you don't have what it takes to be a millionaire, what if it's just a pipe dream. There are a few of us who don't have millionaire mindsets. Does that mean it won't happen for us?

When we pay 1000's of dollars and go to the seminars and listen to the great speeches about wealth and building a financial portfolio, why is it like a foreign language? When we are reaching for success, why is it that we step over people and use people, sabotage people just to climb to the top only to realize if we had stayed with a certain person, business or ministry that that would be the vehicle that would have brought us success. It's a dog-eatdog world when it comes to climbing to the top. It becomes more competitive which is not always a bad thing, but it can become bad when you begin to step over people and dog people out just to be able to succeed.

In this book, you may see the many struggles that I have encountered, and the pit falls and walls I had encountered trying to reach my expected end. When many people questioned as to why I was still with Bishop, I've seen many people come and go come and go. They come with great aspirations and very ambitious for us to only learn that they had other motives and soon moved on to other adventures. They never fully reach their full potential because they didn't stick with it long enough to see the end result.

There is no stress, no distress and it's all because of loyalty and who I'm loyal to.

What has surprised me is nobody saw me at the top. They always saw me assisting, setting up, breaking down, hauling trash, putting up tents, driving the van, cleaning up the church, picking up the mail and so forth. Isn't it funny that while I was doing these things, they were stepping stones to where I had to go? I had to go to all those places to learn all the lessons I had to learn. I could've jumped ship and gone to greener pastures, or I could've stayed and created my own pastures which I chose to do. I stuck with it and now I am surprised about the outcome.

Many people are loyal only when things go their way and as soon as things don't go their way they're ready to pack and leave. If you continue to do this all of your life, you will end up nowhere. It's sad to say that's where many of us are, nowhere. All because we stuck with nothing long enough to see the outcome. We change jobs every month. We change churches every year and expect great things, but it never happens. We expect to have millions, but we're not connected to the people who can teach us and train us how to make and maintain the millions. It's not that I was so smart or so articulate. it was not that I was that popular, but I have what I have today because of one word, loyalty.

Loyalty is the new cash. While people are running around trying to make ends meet trying to figure out how to make it, God has got me in a Secret Place and he's taking care of me. There is no stress, no distress and it's all because of loyalty and who I'm loyal to. Some people are loyal to people who are never going to take them anywhere, and that's sad. You spent all of your life building up someone, investing in someone, and pushing someone who never builds you up, never invested in you and who has never pushed you.

You may have seen this book as a series of lessons and stories of how to persevere in the good times the bad times, to get you to that expected end. For every experience I've been through, I don't regret it because it made me who I am from rejected to respected, to no self-esteem to highly esteemed, from tolerated to celebrated, and from impoverished to obtaining wealth. I want to leave you with this, not all money is cash. Protect your resources because Loyalty is the New Cash.

Contact US

 919.636.0855

 Info@rlkingministries.org

www.rlkingministries.org

RL KING
MINISTRIES

THE KING
and His
GLORY
(PART 2)
MORE GOLD FROM THE BOOK OF ISAIAH
ABOUT THE COMING KING OF GLORY

GREG HARRIS

Never stop Dreaming
IT WILL WORK THIS TIME

LET GO OF THE COOKIES
Do You See What They See In You?

James Edwards

THE LIE
and other
BIBLICAL TRUTHS
from the COMING TRIBULATION

Greg Harris

DELIVERANCE FOR REAL
Dr. Shirley R. Brown, Th.D

WORKBOOK

TEMEILA C. DANIEL

A Guide to Virtual Meeting
NETIQUETTE

GEORGE BLOOMER SCHOOL OF MINISTRY PRESENTS
Warfarecology

ALTARS & UNGODLY COVENANTS

BISHOP GEORGE BLOOMER

S.O.D
SECRETS OF DELIVERANCE
The Bishop's Notes

GEORGE BLOOMER
BEST SELLING AUTHOR OF WITCHCRAFT IN THE PEWS

Miss Carter's HANDWRITING
PRACTICE YOUR
ABC's
AND COLORING BOOK

DOLLETTE CARTER

CPSIA information can be obtained
at www.ICGtesting.com
Printed in the USA
LVHW071500020523
745889LV00023B/1526